The Conscience of a Teacher

Other Titles by Keen Babbage

Extreme Teaching, Second Edition (2014)

Can Schools Survive?: Questions to Ask, Actions to Take (2014)

Teachers Know What Works: Experience, Not Statistics, Confirms What Will Work (2013)

The Power of Middle School: Maximizing These Vital Years (2012)

Reform Doesn't Work: Grassroots Efforts Can Provide Answers to School Improvement (2012)

The Dream and the Reality of Teaching: Becoming the Best Teacher Students Ever Had (2011)

The Extreme Principle: What Matters Most, What Works Best (2010)

Extreme Writing: Discovering the Writer in Every Student (2010)

Extreme Economics: Teaching Children and Teenagers about Money, Second Edition (2007)

Results-Driven Teaching: Teach So Well That Every Student Learns (2006)

Extreme Students: Challenging All Students and Energizing Learning (2005)

Extreme Learning (2004)

Extreme Teaching (2002)

High Impact Teaching: Overcoming Student Apathy (1998)

Meetings for School-Based Decision Making (1997)

911: The School Administrator's Guide to Crisis Management (1996)

The Conscience of a Teacher

More Than Fulfilling a Contract

Keen Babbage

ROWMAN & LITTLEFIELD
Lanham • Boulder • New York • London

Published by Rowman & Littlefield
A wholly owned subsidiary of The Rowman & Littlefield Publishing Group, Inc.
4501 Forbes Boulevard, Suite 200, Lanham, Maryland 20706
www.rowman.com

Unit A, Whitacre Mews, 26-34 Stannary Street, London SE11 4AB

Copyright © 2015 by Keen Babbage

All rights reserved. No part of this book may be reproduced in any form or by any electronic or mechanical means, including information storage and retrieval systems, without written permission from the publisher, except by a reviewer who may quote passages in a review.

British Library Cataloguing in Publication Information Available

Library of Congress Cataloging-in-Publication Data

Library of Congress Cataloging-in-Publication Data Available
ISBN 978-1-4758-1415-6 (cloth) -- ISBN 978-1-4758-1416-3 (pbk.) -- ISBN 978-1-4758-1417-0 (electronic)

To my parents, my grandparents and my great-grandparents; and
To Bob, Laura, Robert, Julie, Brian, and Rudy.

Contents

Preface ix

Introduction 1

1 Purpose as Guidance 5
2 Stop the Nonsense 9
3 Why Teach? 15
4 Protect Instruction 19
5 Build Responsibility 23
6 Challenge Education Reform 27
7 Communicate with Teachers 31
8 Communicate with Administrators 35
9 Keeping Promises 39
10 Self-Honesty 43
11 Pure Law 49
12 Great Examples 53
13 Real People 59
14 Know When 65
15 Mandatory Teaching 69
16 Seek Wise Counsel 75
17 Getting More 81
18 Good News 85
19 Self-Preservation 89

20	The Dictatorship of Data	93
21	Teacher or Administrator?	97
22	Keep Learning	101
23	It Is Personal	105
24	Credit or Discredit?	111
25	Beyond a Job	115
26	Keeping Promises	119
27	Diligent Excellence	123
28	Increasing Complexity	127
29	Not Alone	133
30	Enough?	137

Epilogue: Your Conscience Speaks to You	141
About the Author	143

Preface

This book is written to explore the heart, the soul, the essence of education. When all the confusing and complicating layers of political, bureaucratic, interest group, think tank, social engineering, and other onerous, inefficient, burdensome ordeals are removed from the education empire, the essential core is a classroom where a teacher and students work.

Many variables and factors impact the results in a classroom. A teacher cannot change the accumulated life experiences a student brings. A teacher cannot change the difficult living circumstances that some students face daily. Nonetheless, of all the variables and factors that educators can control, none can match the impact of a capable, determined, skilled, conscientious teacher.

This book explores the conscience of a teacher. This book will include thirty short chapters. Each chapter considers an important topic that relates to the work of a teacher. Insights will include reflections on the professional, ethical, and personal aspects of being a teacher. The reader will encounter hope and inspiration balanced with reality and practicality. Each chapter will stand alone and can be read independently of the others; however, there will be thoughts and ideas that thematically flow throughout the thirty chapters.

The reader is encouraged to reflect upon the content of these chapters and to think for himself or herself. The book is not presented as the final, ultimate, flawless examination of conscience, although there is much insight in these pages; rather, the book enables readers to analyze and then to confirm or to improve the content of it, plus use guidance from their consciences.

The book also initiates thoughts of conscience in general and the application of conscience to teaching in particular. *The Conscience of a Teacher* is intended to inform readers yet also stimulate thought, reflection, ideas, ideals, and certainty.

There are topics of conscience and matters of conscience in addition to those presented in this book. The ideas and the topics presented in this book provide insightful guidance for contemplation about and for actions based on the conscience of a teacher.

The goal of education is to cause learning, but to the teacher in a classroom who is the essential practitioner of education, there are far too many laws, regulations, political actions, mandated tests, think tank pontifications, interest group agendas, foundation social engineering endeavors, bureaucratic mazes, and top-down reforms that counterproductively interfere with teaching and learning.

Recent decades have seen several trends emerge that raise serious concern about the impact those trends are having on schools, on classrooms, on students, on learning, on teaching, on teachers.

The politicalization of education is one such trend. Governments—national, state, and local—seem convinced that the perfect reform, law, regulation, or policy about education, while still elusive, is one executive, legislative, or bureaucratic action away. The result is complication, compromise, confusion, and complexity. One political endeavor designed to fix schools fails, so another political endeavor to finally fix schools is implemented, only to fail.

These repeated political failures should create awareness that the political reform of education does not get the desired result, but instead, the failures bring another reform that also fails. The school reform machine functions perpetually, yet it malfunctions in its ability to truly favorably impact what matters most and what works best in a classroom.

The bureaucratization of education in recent decades results in teachers asking questions such as "Why do we have to change the way we teach writing?," "What was wrong with the old curriculum?," "More tests. Is that possible? How can we teach everything we need to teach and spend four more days on tests the state requires?," "Are you serious? I have to attend a full week of training on the new reading program that every teacher is supposed to implement in every class no matter what the subject? That means my students will get behind while I'm gone. Then we have to spend time on this new program. I'm still implementing two other new programs that started last year. Enough of this nonsense. Please, just let me teach."

Those sincere questions and thoughts raise very valid concerns. Elected officials pass a law. The bureaucratic system writes the regulations to implement the law. The school districts create policies to comply with the law and the regulations. Administrators at schools are told what to do, and then they tell teachers what the new law/regulation/policy language mandates.

One response from teachers is "Why didn't any of those higher-ups ask me? I could have told them why this will never work. I could have given them better ideas that cost less to do, maybe cost nothing to do, and that really work. Who are these people who can't teach but who keep telling me how to teach?"

The gadgetization of education raises concerns. In recent decades our society has benefited in many ways from new technology. We will not return to a society without computers, the Internet, and related machinery or gadgets; however, schools must use technology wisely, not simply because it is new, fancy, neat, interesting, has great graphics, and attracts attention. When affordable technology and the endless variety of electronic gadgets are evaluated as the best way to cause the intended learning, then they should be used. That same filtering and evaluating method applies to all instructional practices or resources.

My parents and my grandparents highly valued education. They closely supervised my work as a student. I knew what their requirements were. They were right, and I benefited from their standards, their encouragement, and their refusal to tolerate excuses. I have no recall of my family ever asking me if I had fun at school. They did ask me daily about what I worked on, what I learned, and what homework I had.

In recent decades an expectation that school needs to be fun has emerged. "How was school?" might be answered with "Not bad. We had fun in science. Math was dull. Math is never any fun." Places of teaching and learning are called schools. They are not called amusement parks. In education, fun can be a by-product of compelling learning that fascinates, but fun is not the goal. How did fun become more important than work, which causes learning?

With such trends and concerns in mind, the astute thinker asks, "How will education improve?" The best answers do not include more laws, more regulations, more policies, more think tank position papers, more interest group agendas, more social engineering, more bureaucracy, more gadgets, or more pursuit of fun.

The best answers will come from the conscience of a teacher. This book is written to pursue those conscientious answers.

History and current practice confirm that the most effective, the highest quality, the most exemplary teaching has always come from the most capable, the most skilled, the most eager to improve, the most results driven, the most conscientious, and the most conscience-driven teachers. The conscience of the best teachers has always insisted on and continues today to insist on superior performance.

The concept of conscience as it relates to being a teacher involves ethics, honor, integrity, duty, principles, virtue, and application of the Golden Rule. The concept of conscience also involves a personal work ethic that far surpasses any employment contractual obligations and requirements.

Conscience also involves a personal code of honorable conduct and actions that far surpass requirements of law, policies, and regulations. Conscience includes knowledge of what is right and what is wrong. Conscience calls for a personal commitment to doing and supporting what is right while avoiding and opposing what is wrong.

The subject of the conscience of a teacher is important because the favorable impact of a conscience-driven teacher is unlimited. That impact far surpasses any limited or unlikely good that might come to education from politics, bureaucracies, laws, regulations, policies, reforms, or social engineering.

Education works best in the classroom of a capable, conscientious, responsible, skilled, constantly improving, results-oriented, conscience-driven teacher. Placing the emphasis in school on what works best and on what matters most can occur by following the leadership provided by the conscience of a teacher. Such conscience-driven leadership is always needed, and perhaps it has never been needed more than now.

Keen Babbage
Lexington, Kentucky
May 2014

Introduction

Every profession, every occupation, every business has people who excel. These people surpass all contractual obligations of their employment. Their personal standards, their personal work ethic, and their determination to achieve inspire them and guide them to advanced levels of accomplishment.

What these superior achievers know is not a set of secrets that are unavailable to everyone else. How these preeminent professionals do their work is also not secretive. They research, they think, they read, they analyze, they study, they obtain wise counsel, they follow excellent examples, they work more hours, they work harder, they work smarter.

The most distinguished of these superior achievers do more than get the most laudable results and the highest amount of results. The most distinguished of these superior achievers do the right work in the right way according to professional codes of conduct, ethical standards, legal necessities, and a personal mandate to far surpass any workplace requirement.

The highest achievers, the most productive workers, and the most honorable employees are conscience driven. Doing anything other than superior work is unthinkable to them, it is unacceptable to them, it is immoral to them, it is unprofessional to them, it is unethical to them. They are not driven by contractual obligations. They are conscience driven by an internal insistence to excel properly.

Education has many teachers who are conscience driven to excel properly. Those most honorable people are the foundation of a school. Those distinguished people are the teachers who students identify as the most effective and the most influential. Those respected, virtuous, noble teachers make extraordinary learning happen in the minds of their students.

Please think of the best teacher you ever had. Get a clear, vivid, exact mental picture of a day when you were a student of that teacher. Now, identify what that teacher did to earn the acclaim you are giving to him or her. You are not thinking, "She did exactly what her contract required." You are not thinking, "He never got in trouble with the principal."

You are thinking of inspiring memories such as: "She challenged me." "He never gave up on me." "She refused to accept anything that was less than my best." "He showed me how important it was to learn." "She was so enthusiastic that I got interested." "He made learning so real for me I could finally see what all of this stuff meant for me."

Those dearly remembered teachers far surpassed their contractual obligations. Rather than merely or barely fulfilling the terms of an employment contract, these exemplary teachers fully fulfilled the terms of a contract they have with their conscience.

Their conscience-driven contract does not obligate them to seek an impossible result causing their days to be filled with failure and frustration. Their conscience guides them, sustains them, reminds them, inspires them, and holds them accountable. Their conscience tells them to find a proper way to cause learning for the students in their classroom. Their conscience applauds their good work, yet also expresses dissatisfaction if work is not up to the highest standards. The applause is encouraging. The dissatisfaction is all it takes to correct any flaw.

During my many years as a student in kindergarten through high school, in college and in graduate school, I was blessed to have many conscience-driven teachers. During my thirty years as an educator I have known many colleagues who were conscience-driven teachers. In my work as a teacher or as a school administrator, it has been my intention each day to do much more than and to do much better than fulfill the terms of my employment contract. I require myself to meet the contract terms of my conscience. When that happens the results are magnificent.

"We used to do better with education," I said to a colleague. She completely agreed. We discussed the invasion of schools by education reform acts of aggression, the destructive impact of endless government-required tests, the increasing social media or part-time job distractions that consume student time, the declining work ethic of a growing number of students, and the use of schools to address noneducational societal goals.

Perhaps some of those detrimental trends can be reversed, yet some of those adverse trends may worsen. A conscience-driven teacher can still get beneficial and promising results in his or her classroom. Without those harmful trends and factors, teaching would be less of a steep, uphill climb, but it would be demanding nonetheless. Great teaching is very challenging no matter what obstacles exist, and there are always obstacles.

In my career I have seen school reforms come, go, and come back. Most of those efforts did more harm than good. I have seen bureaucracies force destructive actions on schools. I have repeatedly asked people in authority to listen to teachers so the classroom reality can be known completely before any decisions are made or before any actions are taken. School reforms continue. Bureaucratic mandates continue. The lack of genuine listening continues.

Despite all of that, conscience-driven teachers continue to cause learning, to touch lives, to make a difference, to excel.

The conscience of a teacher is a powerful force. The good results obtained can surpass the impact of school reforms, bureaucratic mandates, social engineering, and other specious, delusive, misleading actions.

This book acknowledges the vital importance of and the unlimited beneficial power of the conscience of a teacher. This book gives the reader an opportunity to examine his or her conscience.

The sign in my classroom reminds students that everything said and done in class must be "G-rated, legal, and ethical." That standard helps establish a goal for our classroom conscience. The conscience of a teacher can lead the way to great teaching, great learning, and a conscientious learning community.

School reforms and other manipulations of education are temporal, temporary, and tepid. Conscience-driven teaching causes learning—it always has and it always will. This book advances the timeless truths of the conscience of a teacher. This book also applies the conscience of a teacher to specific topics, actions, issues, questions, and situations.

Conscience—a core knowledge of right versus wrong; an inner voice of ethics, of integrity, of honor, of virtue—when applied to teaching is transforming. Conscientious, honorable, just, true guidance from deep within the heart and soul can far surpass mandated external directives that seek to impact education from the outside.

The essential work of education is done within classrooms. Essential guidance for how to most effectively and most conscientiously do that work can come from the strong, well-developed conscience of a teacher.

Chapter One

Purpose as Guidance

A teacher looks at the students in her classroom and says to herself, "Every decision I make, every action I take as the teacher of these students will include this thought—if my children, my son and my daughter, were in a classroom, what would I hope the teacher would do for them?"

This teacher knows that her students are not her actual family, yet if she provides an educational experience for her students that has the quality of the educational experience she desires for her own children, the results can be superior.

No employment contract for a teacher will require that students are taught as if they are the actual offspring of the teacher. How could the actions, the thoughts, or the motives of the teacher as parent be measured objectively and by the few moments, possibly a few hours, of classroom observation by a school administrator, which commonly forms an evaluation of teachers?

There is merit in a teacher asking himself or herself, "Am I doing everything for my students that I expect the teachers of my children to do for them?" This type of thinking is an extension of the Golden Rule, which calls for treating other people the way we hope to be treated. Such a standard far surpasses what an employment contract requires. Such a standard comes from the heart, the soul, and the conscience of an exemplary teacher.

What is the purpose of a school? Consider that question and develop an answer. A clearly identified purpose provides comprehensive guidance. A certain purpose can function as a filter through which proper actions flow and by which unacceptable actions are blocked.

The purpose of a school is to cause learning. Different responses to the question "What is the purpose of a school?" will have various words, but the essential idea that unites all valid statements of school purpose is the complete commitment to and the complete concentration on learning.

The purpose of a school being clearly stated gives exact guidance to a teacher. While grading papers, while planning lessons, during the school day when students are with the teacher in a classroom, when a teacher participates with colleagues in a meeting, when a teacher communicates with parents or guardians of students, the statement of school purpose guides all actions.

"Am I causing learning? Are the instructional activities I am planning going to cause the most learning and the best learning? Am I causing learning with the comments I am writing on the student essays I am grading? As my colleagues and I make decisions about the school budget, about professional development programs, about approving or rejecting field trip requests, are our decisions going to lead to actions that most effectively cause learning?"

The conscience of a teacher includes other questions. "If my children attended this school, would I be satisfied with the classroom instruction being provided? Would I approve of the school budget in terms of how it impacts my children? Would I be pleased with the individualized comments written by teachers on the papers my children wrote? Would I want my children to go on field trips rather than have classroom instruction?"

A teacher's employment contract could have language in it that requires that "all tests, projects, homework, in-class work, and anything else that is to be graded by the teacher must be fully evaluated, returned to the student within two weeks of receipt by the teacher, and must have a grade entered in the computer within three weeks of receipt of the work by the teacher."

Such a requirement is unacceptable as a standard for any conscientious teacher. A two-week separation between when students turn in work and when students receive that graded work drastically reduces the learning that occurs with swift, complete grading. Thoroughly and promptly grading student work means it can be returned to students while the work is still on their minds, is still fresh in their memory, and is still meaningful.

The conscience of a conscientious teacher is offended by and aggrieved by a nonstandard of returning work to students in two weeks. The conscientious teacher sets a much more honorable standard with guidance from the questions, "For the most and the best learning to be caused, by when will I require myself to have papers thoroughly graded, returned to students, with grades entered in the computer?" and, "When do I expect my children to receive their thoroughly graded papers from their teachers?"

Would it be acceptable to that teacher for his or her children to wait two weeks before their papers were returned and to wait three weeks until grades were entered in the computer providing updated grade information to the student and to the student's parent or guardian? No. The same expectations and standards that a teacher has for the teachers of his or her children need to be met or surpassed by that teacher for his or her students. The conscience of a teacher requires that the most honorable path is chosen rather than the limited work level that barely meets the minimum requirements of an employment contract.

What are other exact actions that the conscience of a teacher compels a conscientious teacher to take or to not take? Think of the best teachers you ever had. Reflect upon those masters of teaching who properly stood out during your years as a student in elementary school, middle school, high school, college, and graduate school.

What did those superior teachers do day to day in their classrooms that so effectively and favorably impacted you? What actions did they consistently do that clearly caused learning? What did they do differently from average teachers or below-average teachers? What actions did they never do that average teachers did often and that below-average teachers did always?

What inspired, motivated, provoked, led those superior teachers to do exemplary work? Did the principal spend more time in their classroom enforcing all mandates? No, the principal probably spent minimal or zero time in such classrooms. Was the teacher competing for an award or a prize? No, there are few such formal acknowledgments for teachers.

Those superior educators were conscience driven. They required of themselves far more than their employment contract mandated, much more than the teacher evaluation checklist with bureaucratic verbosity sought to enforce, and significantly more than was needed to avoid being fired.

They caused learning. They taught with the enthusiasm, the creativity, the resolve, the leadership, the management, the endurance, the persistence, and the devotion that shapes all greatness in any human endeavor. They were guided by the voice of their conscience that included the power of virtue, of ethics, of honor, of duty, of work ethic, of integrity.

Their standard operating procedure was to find a proper way to get results. Their goal was not to finish the day or to get through the school year. Their goals included making every minute count, causing learning continuously by each student, and constantly improving.

Conscientious teachers surpass their employment contract. Conscientious teachers are directed by and accountable to a contract with their conscience that, in truth, is as much or more an imperative covenant as it is a contract.

Of course, conscience-driven teachers abide by all legal and professional terms of their work contract. There is never an issue about obedience to specific requirements such as time of arrival at school, allowed time to leave school at the end of a day, completion of professional development hours, or compliance with directives from the school principal. Yet such efforts are not the completion of the work of a conscientious teacher. Those efforts are procedural processes that the school or the school district insists upon for the functioning of the organization.

Superior teachers require themselves to be much more than organizational functionaries. Superior teachers, conscientious teachers, conscience-driven teachers expect themselves to make a difference, to touch lives, to cause learning, and to work as a teacher with the unlimited devotion they would have if their own children were students in the classroom.

These honorable teachers give themselves the precious gift of knowing they did everything possible to cause learning. They will be able to forever cherish the joys of a meaningful career and of a peaceful soul. They will maximize achievements, and they will minimize regrets.

Why would a conscience-driven teacher have any regrets? Reasons include students who refuse to do any work, political and bureaucratic invasions of schools, inept school administrators, and out-of-touch school district or state education officials. Perhaps all occupations have such factors that no one worker can correct, yet in the area that any one worker can impact, the worker determines the quality of that impact. Conscientious teachers bring the best quality of work to their classroom despite many obstacles, challenges, and difficulties.

Conscience. Purpose. Conscience driven. Conscientious. Honor. Integrity. Virtue. Ethics. Character. Covenant. Work ethic. Duty. Causing learning. Getting results. Eliminating excuses. Surpassing the employment contract. Abiding by the conscience contract. Those are among the admirable, exemplary, and superior factors within the proper conscience of a teacher.

Chapter Two

Stop the Nonsense

New teachers and relatively new teachers can be perplexed when they hear experienced teachers refer to some innovation that has to be implemented as "just one more certain-to-fail scheme that politicians or bureaucrats or other people who are far away from schools are forcing us to do in our classrooms."

The younger teachers may wonder how the older teachers became cynical about school reforms, new ideas, major initiatives, bold transformations, and other highly touted changes. The older teachers would claim that instead of being cynical, they are realistic. Also, they are listening to their conscience.

The conscience of a teacher expresses that there is no time to waste on nonsense, and there is no money to waste on nonsense. The available time and money must be applied to doing what works best and what matters most. Despite the wise insights of a teacher's conscience, there will be more nonsense imposed on education.

What is a conscientious teacher to do amid a continuous infiltration of nonsense coming from school district officials, state or national government education bureaucrats, politicians, interest groups, think tanks, and other individuals or organizations that seek to impact schools?

First, properly comply with the requirements of policies, regulations, and laws. Such compliance is a professional obligation.

Second, do everything else that is good, helpful, instructional, inspiring, and beneficial for your students that you have always done and are still allowed to do.

Third, be heard. It is possible that the people who promote nonsense actually think they are being supportive of education. Help them understand what schools truly need and what schools truly do not need. They may listen and apply your insights. They may listen and ignore your insights. They may not listen, but it is still honorable to provide them with the wisdom about school that can come only from teachers who exclusively know what today's classroom reality is.

Decision makers in the education hierarchy spend little or no time in classrooms. Yet these people are certain that "our schools can do much better. We have several major initiatives that have been approved for immediate implementation. Finally, the high quality of education that has been sought for years will be achieved."

In a few years those major initiatives will have failed only to be followed by more major initiatives that will fail. In the midst of these invasive initiatives, a conscientious teacher must continue to cause learning in addition to meeting all demands of the unproductive initiatives, reforms, innovations, and programs.

Why do political systems impose reforms on education? Reforms, new laws, new regulations, and new policies are the tools that political systems have to use. When education seems to be inadequate, the political process takes the actions it has available; however, no political system, no reform, no law, no regulation, no policy educates students. Teachers are in the position from which students can be educated and through which learning can be caused.

Perennial yet temporary and transient reforms of education will continue and will breed successive reforms. They are often nuisances, obstacles, and barriers; however, they are not insurmountable. Endure the reforms, obey the laws that reforms impose, follow the regulations and policies that emerge from reforms, but do much more than the reforms require.

Reforms of education do not cause learning. Reforms that flow from the political and bureaucratic processes do not educate students. Reforms restructure education, revise the curriculum, change the teacher evaluation system, and create new processes, systems, and procedures.

Comply with the reforms as law, policy, and regulation requires, but do much more. Teach your students. Cause your students to learn. Listen to and follow your conscience to implement a true reform of education as you do what matters most and do what works best.

The conscience of a teacher is anguished by, but never defeated by, the never-ending nonsense. There are training sessions to attend, so the latest and worst method for teaching writing can be presented. There are meetings to attend about the most recent teacher evaluation system—let's see, that makes five different evaluation systems during the past twenty-one years despite the fact that the essential aspects of great teaching have not changed.

There are changes to the curriculum every few years despite the few substantial changes in knowledge. Perhaps there is a curriculum-changing company or a covert curriculum-innovation industry that profits from such revisions, which often are heavy on rhetoric, flow charts, new terminology, or hidden motives, and are quite light on new meaningful content.

The conscientious teacher will continue to cause learning. The conscientious teacher will magnificently direct, lead, manage, and control all that he or she is allowed to direct, lead, manage, and control. Despite relentless attempts by misguided or poorly informed people to make classrooms and schools into robotic assembly lines where education is somehow mechanically produced through contrived procedures, the conscientious teacher can prevail and must prevail. The conscientious teacher is each student's best hope for a highly effective educational experience.

The conscience of a teacher does not look for battles. The conscientious teacher knows not to quixotically confront superpowers in lost causes. A teacher's concentration is on causing learning to be experienced by students in a classroom. When the political process or the bureaucratic educational hierarchy considers actions or takes actions that are harmful to teaching and learning, the conscience of a teacher is distressed and senses a need to speak up.

Separate harmful nonsense from that which is irritating yet does no damage. Challenge and confront the worst of the nonsense. Team up with other conscientious teachers to more forcefully challenge and confront the worst of the nonsense. Keep teaming up so the rest of the nonsense is also questioned.

A conscientious teacher longs for schools and school districts to be no-nonsense places, organizations, and systems. They should be nonsense-free, but they are polluted by and compromised by harmful, counterproductive, irrational, mischievous nonsense. Perhaps all organizations have some degree of the nonsensical.

A teacher can seek to make his or her classroom a no-nonsense zone. Concentrating on this rewarding, important, needed, and vital possibility may be the best way to counter the political and bureaucratic nonsense that increasingly attacks schools from within the education empire and from without the education empire.

Not all ideas, mandates, proposals, laws, policies, regulations, or initiatives from the political structure, from the bureaucracy, from education officials, and from various groups that seek to impact education are nonsense, but some are. To a teacher who deals all day, every day with the reality of causing learning with each student in a classroom, it can seem that most actions or ideas from people outside of the classroom are nonsense, are invasive, are interfering, are not needed, are harmful, and are burdens that further complicate the already demanding work of a teacher.

The conscience of a teacher uses a precise nonsense filter. This intellectual filtration system thrives on the questions "Is the instruction plan I am preparing for my students the best way to cause the desired learning?" and "Is this how I hope my own children are taught?" The answer has to be *yes*, or a conscientious teacher will change the instructional plan to make it the best or will replace the initial plan altogether with one that is the best.

Conscientious teachers long for the day when education decision makers and other influential people throughout the education empire of politicians, bureaucrats, education administrators, colleges of education, think tanks, interest groups, and others will use the nonsense filter also. One way those groups could use the nonsense filter would be to present any education-related idea they are considering to a large number of teachers, who can provide the nonsense filtration insights and accuracy that classroom teachers have unique skill with.

Alas, it is likely that nonsensical ideas, laws, regulations, and policies will continue to be approved and implemented. For people who contemplate why educational results in the United States do not always surpass educational results in other nations, one answer could be the obstruction to learning that nonsensical mandates on schools impose in this country.

Amid the steady stream of nonsensical, harmful, counterproductive mandates that are imposed on schools, what can a conscientious teacher do to properly comply with the required mandates yet still cause learning in the best possible way for his or her students?

Look for flexibility and options within the mandate. Does the requirement state that students will understand the constitutional structure of the legislative, executive, and judicial branches of the U.S. government, or does the requirement specify exactly how students are to be taught—what materials will be used, what activities will be completed, what tests will be taken, what projects will be turned in?

If there is flexibility in how the teaching is done, then a teacher can use his or her knowledge of the students and experience with a variety of instructional methods to cause the desired learning.

If there are specified instructional activities that must be completed, find out if it is permissible to do those compulsory tasks as part of what is done. If the answer is yes, then the teacher can add the better instructional activities to effectively supplement the mandated work.

Upon deciding to become a teacher, it is highly unlikely that any aspiring teachers chose this profession because they would get to spend their career automatically, mechanistically, and robotically carrying out nonsensical mandates, requirements, directives, policies, laws, and regulations.

Similarly, experienced educators do not remain in the teaching profession because they get to carry out such nonsense. The most conscience driven of aspiring teachers and of experienced teachers expect themselves to cause learning, to touch lives, to make a difference in the majestic movement known as education.

Do not despair. Although the demanding work of a teacher will be made more complicated by perennial invasions of nonsense, you can rise above that interference by looking deeply into your heart, your mind, your conscience.

Obeying the laws, policies, regulations, and other mandates is a professional obligation and is a contractual duty. Doing much more than that and doing much better than that so you can cause learning for each student as if all students are your children being taught as you desire your own children to be taught—that standard comes from the conscience of a teacher.

Perhaps the nonsense will never stop. Be prepared for more nonsense. Also be prepared and be relentlessly devoted to minimizing the impact of the nonsense while maximizing the guidance of the wisdom that comes from your conscience.

Oppose nonsense, but as nonsense endures, outsmart the nonsense. Let good sense prevail. Let the good sense that emerges from the conscience of a conscientious teacher triumph.

Chapter Three

Why Teach?

The purpose of a school is to cause learning. The people in education who can have the most substantial, effective, and direct impact on the attainment of and realization of that purpose are teachers; therefore, the reason to teach is to cause learning.

If aspiring teachers and current teachers are asked "Why teach?" the wording of the replies would vary, but the fundamental, uniting theme of the answers should express a dedication to the goal of causing learning.

The conscience of a teacher is steadfastly true to the essential responsibility of causing learning. Conscientious teachers evaluate themselves with much higher requirements than the official observation checklist used by school administrators during their limited visits into the classroom.

The once-in-a-long-while formal classroom observation by a school administrator may include a lengthy list of teacher standards, ideals, actions, practices, and exemplars for the administrator to check as observed or not observed. Some written comments could be added.

The conscience-driven teacher uses a shorter evaluation process, which asks, "Am I causing the most possible learning for all students in the best possible ways?" and "Am I teaching the way I hope my own children are being taught?" The most compelling, honorable, ethical, and genuine reason to teach is to get great results in the place where the real person-to-person work is done that causes learning.

It is improper to become a teacher for warped motives, such as not having to go to work in the summer or because the real goal is to be a coach and that involves having to teach. Specious, deceptive, deluding rationalizations demean the person doing such unethical nonthinking. If such mental mischief leads a misplaced person into the teaching profession, the distorted motives of the imitation teacher will be harmful to students. That person should select another career where a complete, sincere, certain commitment can be made so the work is done well, so the worker is effective, and so people impacted by the worker are given their due.

It is unreasonable, illogical, and unethical to seek employment as a teacher if your commitment is incomplete. The work of a teacher is done well only when the dedication to the work is equal to the realistic requirements of the work. Why put yourself through ten months of misery, frustration, and failure each year to get two summer months when you are not required to report for work? Why put students through that?

If causing learning in the minds of students is your career objective; if you can fully and skillfully do the work that causes the desired learning; if you are able and willing to cope with the nonsense (please see chapter 2) that is imposed on schools; and if no other work so inspires you, attracts you, applies your talents, and evokes your complete commitment, you and teaching could be a thoroughly symbiotic match.

Schools that have clubs need teachers to sponsor those organizations. Schools with athletic teams need teachers to coach those groups. A conscientious sponsor or coach will complete those extracurricular duties effectively, but never at the expense of classroom teaching, and never with more effort or dedication than classroom duties are given.

The conscience-driven teacher says, "I am a teacher first and a sponsor or coach second. I am a teacher who also coaches a team or sponsors a club, but my highest obligation is to our school's highest priority—causing learning by students in classrooms."

Is it possible to be overly optimistic about what can be accomplished during a career as a teacher? That question deserves serious consideration so that a collision with reality is avoided.

People who are motivated to teach for all of the right reasons—such as to cause learning, to touch lives, to make a difference, to be for students the significant source of guidance and inspiration that their teachers were for them—must also be bluntly aware of and ruggedly prepared for the increasingly discouraging, frustrating, and complicating realities that face teachers. These realities include the following:

1. Lethargic, disinterested, lazy students. Decreasing work ethic in a growing number of students. Refusal to seriously read by more and more students. Addiction to social media, which consumes several hours daily by many students. Part-time jobs for high school students to whom school is an inconvenient interference with their work schedule.
2. Students who imitate the crude, vulgar, immoral, mean, uncivilized misbehavior, language, and attitudes that are glorified in some of or

much of popular culture's music, television programs, video games, movies, celebrities, and Internet websites.
3. Students who refuse to do any work. Students who rarely or never turn in homework. Students whose daily plan at school is to eat breakfast, eat lunch, skip class, and then steal from the students who behave properly and work properly.
4. Other teachers who tolerate unacceptable behavior in their classrooms rather than dealing with those improper actions. The disobedient student then comes to your class daily with the attitude of, habit of, and actions of defiance and disruption.
5. School administrators who do not effectively discipline students. To avoid having high numbers of out-of-school suspensions at their school, some administrators use empty, ineffective, nondiscipline alternatives that the students interpret as meaning they completely got away with the school crime they committed. Beware: rarely is school misbehavior called a crime even when the same wrongdoing elsewhere in the community would be dealt with as a crime. This may impact the safety of people who work at school and the safety of properly behaved students at school.
6. Changes—not necessarily improvements—each year in procedures at school; in the required testing system at school; in how writing is taught; in the use of technology; in the student code of conduct; in allowed student use of cell phones; in the number of activities that students are permitted/encouraged to attend during school days, thus missing class time; in record keeping that must be maintained; in the number of meetings that must be attended; and in mandates imposed by local school districts, state governments, and the national government.
7. The many hours beyond the school day needed to prepare lessons and grade papers. The unreasonable requests made of you, such as "Please schedule a time when Alice can take her final exam one day after school. She will be out of town during the week the school has final exams." That means that for academic security reasons a separate exam must be created for Alice, and time for her to take the exam must be found. You must accommodate the directive of the family, which your principal approved with no regard for the impact on you and with no acknowledgment of your extra effort.

People who go into teaching for the right reasons and who stay in the teaching profession for the right reasons need to know that they will be working with some adults who are teachers, school administrators, education bureaucrats, or otherwise impacting education who are led by the wrong reasons. That mixture of motives can create a gridlock leading to frustration, confusion, and regret.

People who become teachers for the right reasons owe themselves a reality check. How resilient will you be when your optimism, determination, dedication, extra work hours, and total devotion to teaching collide with lazy colleagues, an inept school administrator, vulgar and incorrigible students whose crude language is repeatedly directed at you in person, parents and guardians who make excuses for their children or who falsely blame you and take their animosity to the authorities, a person being selected for an administrative position that includes evaluating you yet that person was the least qualified of all candidates for the position? How was that person chosen? In education, as in some other fields, decision-making friends take care of job-seeking friends without consideration of qualifications sometimes.

If you are absolutely aware of the realities faced by teachers, and if you are absolutely relentless, uncompromisingly devoted to causing learning, and you are equipped with the skills to cause learning, you could be an outstanding teacher.

Why teach? Because no other work so compels your heart, mind, and soul. Because you have the necessary skills. Because no other work matters as much to you. Because you and teaching are a perfect match for all of the right reasons.

Why teach? Because you care, and you will cause learning. Because everything you do as a teacher will be as if the students are your own children. Because teaching needs you and you need teaching. Because you chose teaching and teaching equally chose you in a true covenant that far surpasses a contract.

Please know that despite superficial platitudes spoken by noneducators about "teaching is the most important profession in our nation," our society often acts differently than those words suggest.

Also know that while altruism, benevolence, humanitarianism, compassion, beneficence, and crusading missionary zeal can motivate a person to select teaching as a career, the actual work of teaching can often exhaust and sometimes thwart the most earnest, the most inspired, the most resolute teacher. Successfully teaching is a vastly arduous, exacting, laborious, and strenuous endeavor. Idealism alone is insufficient to guarantee effective work by a teacher. Be aware of and cope with these stark realities as you hold on to the glorious possibilities of teaching.

Chapter Four

Protect Instruction

Causing learning requires an abundance of time. The time that teachers and students spend on classroom instruction must be stubbornly, uncompromisingly, nobly defended and protected. Conscience-driven teachers refuse to yield instructional time to noninstructional thieves of school time.

Why would anyone steal instructional time? Apparently, there are many motives for such theft, but there are no convincing reasons.

Various community organizations have goals and objectives that can relate to people who are in the age groups of students in elementary school, middle school, or high school. These organizations may offer lofty concepts to school district officials and/or to school administrators explaining why their presentation to students would be beneficial.

Such groups may contend that what they offer schools matches precisely with some aspects of the official curriculum; therefore, the time devoted to students attending the group's presentation at school enhances education. At this point the school district official or the school administrator hearing the sales pitch from the community group must think as a conscientious teacher thinks.

"If we allow one community group to meet with students about some local government physical fitness initiative and we let the local bankers association make a series of presentations about financial literacy and we let our elementary schools recruit high school students to come mentor fourth-graders during occasional school days and we send big groups of students to the local college 'Careers in Science' event, that will reduce time teachers have for classroom instruction. Plus, there are dozens of other similar requests. The answer is no. Class time will not be sacrificed. Those other activities have to take place outside of the school day."

Some school district officials and school administrators such as principals or assistant principals may never think as conscience-driven teachers think. Perhaps those officials and administrators are so removed from the classroom that they have no awareness of the importance of each hour of instructional time. Perhaps the officials and administrators who used to be teachers were not conscientious teachers who protected and used each minute of classroom instructional time, or perhaps they have lost that earlier edge.

Those officials and administrators may see personal, career, or political advantages if they approve the requests of community groups for use of classroom instructional time to advance the goals, agenda, and objectives of such groups. The private ambitions, the forging of political coalitions, the trading of favors may motivate school district officials and school administrators to approve many requests by community groups seeking to stage and exhibit their ideas, their recruitment efforts, their information, and even their propaganda.

Conscience-driven teachers individually may be unable to reverse the inclination of their management colleagues; however, conscience-driven teachers collectively could have more impact. Use the methods available to communicate the urgency of protecting classroom instructional time. When a school has a decentralized decision-making process, system, or council or advisory board, conscientious teachers can and must actively, persistently, and continuously be involved.

Within a school there can be efforts, well intentioned or not, to misappropriate classroom instructional time. One teacher schedules a field trip that causes students to miss the classes of other teachers. What makes the field trip teacher's work more important than the work of the other teachers who never take field trips out of respect to the class time allocated to each teacher and because they realize that the inefficiency of field trips—getting to the destination, returning from the destination, monitoring everyone, planning, follow-up, paperwork—is not justified, especially when virtual field trips can be created in the classroom through creative instruction?

"Why do teachers have to make so much effort to protect instructional time? Isn't instruction what schools are supposed to do? Why would schools let anything get in the way of properly using the time that is scheduled for classroom instruction?"

Those are reasonable questions, logical questions, insightful questions. One answer is that schools can stray from their purpose. Another answer is that the education empire's bureaucracy is out of touch with classrooms. Another answer can be the duplicitous actions of any manipulating, misleading, misguided people in power throughout the education hierarchy.

What is to be done? Protect instruction. Make every minute count in your classroom. Some of those minutes will be stolen from you for a variety of reasons, most of which are unacceptable, specious, or just plain wrong. That reality is frustrating and disappointing to a conscientious teacher. It is demoralizing to realize that some actions are taken that sabotage your efforts to cause learning.

In the time you do have with your students in your classroom, relentlessly concentrate all effort toward causing learning. Despite all of the interruptions, distractions, diversions, and counterproductive mandates that steal instructional time, a conscience-driven teacher can, will, and must cause learning. More learning would be caused without the sabotage coming from outside of your classroom, but you can maximize the time and the other resources you do have.

"It's been a long week. It's Friday. We'll just watch a bunch of videos today."

"I'm running late, maybe I can just copy a lot of worksheets and keep them busy today."

"They keep asking for a free day. I could just let them play with their cell phones quietly today."

All of those options are absolutely unacceptable to the conscience of a teacher. A conscientious teacher will not think those thoughts. Those actions would cause no learning. Those actions would waste time. Those actions would diminish the integrity of teaching. Those actions are inherently rejected as evil, as corruption, as delusions. Those actions are never in the mind-set of a conscientious teacher who always protects instruction.

Causing learning requires the protection of instruction against all invasions, enemies, intruders, or deceptions. That sounds so serious and uncompromising. Exactly right. We are not dealing with good enough, with just getting by, with the lowest acceptable effort. We are dealing with honor, virtue, integrity. We are dealing with the conscience, where the standards are exemplary and from which come the most outstanding results.

Chapter Five

Build Responsibility

A high school football team experienced an extremely close, competitive, thrilling game. The score was tied 7 to 7. The score was tied again at 14–14 and then at 21–21.

When time ran out, the score was 28 to 27. The losing team actually had accumulated more yards from passing, more yards from rushing, fewer fumbles, fewer interceptions, and fewer yards in penalties than the winning team had.

Imagine a player from the losing team asking the head referee, "Sir, our team was on top in all of the statistics. You know, rushing yards, passing yards, and lots of other stuff. Can we get two extra credit points for all of those things we did well? Two extra credit points would make us the winner, 29 to 28. Please, sir."

The answer, of course, is no. There is no extra credit in high school football. There is no extra credit in any high school sport. There is no extra credit in high school band, orchestra, or chorus competitions. The results in these events and in other activities are determined by what is earned.

If a team or another school group did not win an event, game, competition, or match, they can improve if they accept responsibility for their performance. Extra credit should not rescue them when they come in second place or worse. Responsibility, hard work, correcting mistakes, additional practice, and strengthened commitment can lead toward a better likelihood of victory in the next event.

In the classroom, students sometimes or often seek extra credit. "My grade is so low in this class. I did really bad on some tests, and there are two projects I never did. What could I do for some extra credit?"

What is the answer to that question that would be the reply that most communicates discipline, honor, virtue, ethics, integrity, and conscientiousness? Consider the following possible responses:

1. "Extra credit? Sure. You can do some reports and worksheets. You are barely passing the class, but do these ten worksheets and write a report about something we discussed. That will bring up the grade."
2. "There is an optional project you could do to get part of the points for one of the projects you never did. The optional project takes much more work and earns fewer points than the original project, but it is better than a zero grade. Each of those projects were worth 100 points. You could get up to 50 points on the optional project so that turns one zero grade into a 50 if you do great work."
3. "There is no extra credit in this class. We said that on the first day of the year. Your grade is what you earn. We have several more tests and one or two more projects. Do A-quality work on those and you will improve your grade. You could have done A-quality work before now, but there's still time to work hard and increase your grade, but there is no extra credit. You knew that."

Which of the above responses most effectively, most honestly, and most realistically builds responsibility? The third response best builds responsibility and also includes a lesson about discipline and work, plus reality.

"Why not let the students do some extra credit? What difference does it make if they did the projects a few months ago or if they do a lot of new work right now? It's all the same type of work, isn't it?"

No, it is not all equivalent work. For a student who consistently has a failing grade during a semester or during a school year, the grade indicates that the student has accomplished very little. A sudden surge of projects and paperwork cannot replace the learning that the student rejected for months.

Learning accumulates when education is most productively, fruitfully, logically, and potently designed. Today's instructional activity builds upon the foundation of yesterday's learning. The student who is allowed to do extra credit work that places a temporary bandage over a learning injury is a student who escapes the realities of responsibility.

Work must be turned in when it is due. The clock ticks in a basketball game played by elementary school students, middle school students, or high school students. When the last second ticks away and no time remains, the game ends and the score stands as it is. No extra credit points are available. No extra time can be added.

Students who participate in extracurricular activities learn that more work can create desired results, but that extra credit is nonexistent. The classroom should apply the same reality and teach the same lesson.

In recent decades, concerns have been expressed about grade inflation. The schoolwork done today by students who get a grade of A is work that, according to grade inflation whistle-blowers, would have earned a grade of B or C in an earlier era. Extra credit is one fuel of grade inflation.

Extra credit also fosters a false appearance of accomplishment. The grade a student is given based on extra credit conveys that more learning took place than actually did occur. Why mislead the student with a fictional grade? Why promote cutting corners or an easy way out instead of promoting steady, consistent, habitual acceptance of responsibility and the true achievement that comes from continuous, conscientious work? (See chapter 24 for more about extra credit.)

The conscience-driven work ethic and work standards of a conscientious teacher can help students see, understand, and more fully develop their own conscientiousness. Anything less from teachers could be followed by less responsibility by and from students.

It has become increasingly common, perhaps due to political correctness or perhaps due to a decline in overall societal standards of proper behavior, for students who violate rules, instructions, or laws to be told "You made a bad choice." Contrast that comment with this statement: "What you did was wrong." What message is communicated by each of those conclusions?

If behavior is on a continuum of choices, are there shades of very bad, bad, somewhat bad, almost bad, a little bad, in between bad and good, rising to a little good, almost good, somewhat good, good, or very good? Does such a continuum create confusion and imprecision? Does such a range suggest that certainty in identifying correct behavior can vary across people or among various situations?

When a student hears that what he or she did was wrong, there is a more clear, precise, and exact distinction between what is wrong and what is right. When a student is told that his or her action was wrong, it can help establish a more certain awareness that a slight correction of or a slight change of behavior is insufficient. The student is being told that he or she has the responsibility to do what is right, to be right, to act rightly because it is right. Rightness has inherent merit, worth, value, goodness, and benefits.

Doing what is wrong is worse than making a bad choice. It is supporting what is wrong through intentional action.

Doing what is right is better than making a good choice. It is supporting what is right through intentional action.

A commitment to accepting the responsibility to do what is right contains an enduring bond with rightness. Fluctuations between good choices and bad choices can be replaced by a permanent commitment to what is right.

A conscience-driven teacher is guided in all decisions and in all actions by the fundamental dedication to doing what is right. This dedication is revealed throughout each day in the classroom as the conscientious teacher exemplifies what is right and in so doing teaches what is right. These teachers build responsibility one moment at a time, one assignment at a time, one lesson at a time, one student at a time as individual direction is needed and, ideally, within all students at all times.

Perfection will not be attained, but the pursuit of perfection increases the possibility of actually attaining superior, near-perfect results. Why pursue less? Why build less? Responsibility can be built. Build. Build more. Keep building.

Chapter Six

Challenge Education Reform

Absolute adherence to the purpose of a school by everyone at the school will create the manifestation of that purpose. Conscience-guided teachers design and direct all of their actions to consistently implement the school purpose, which is to cause learning. The result is that learning is caused. Schools should be decisively about learning the curriculum content.

In recent decades schools have been inundated with a deluge of education reforms. The chronically incorrect premise is that because schools have not solved every issue, educational and others, that students in kindergarten through high school face, the schools are failing; therefore, mandated changes must be imposed on schools.

Conscientious teachers do not need political, bureaucratic, top-down school reforms with the typical curriculum changes, new testing systems, endless and pointless professional development, a new teacher evaluation system, and a variety of new teaching methods that must be quickly implemented before the new testing system begins.

Conscience-driven teachers are the ultimate education reform because they do what works. They do not need directives from bureaucrats, political misdirections, think tank paid policy proposals, or the narrow agendas of interest groups interfering with the honorable, productive work of conscientious teachers. Nonetheless, the education reform industry keeps manufacturing new reforms to replace the most recently failed reform.

Within the accepted methods of professional protocol, conscientious teachers need to respond when school reform efforts begin to develop and need to lead the opposition to reform ideas that will not work. Their conscience requires that they make the effort to prevent—or limit if that is all that can be achieved—the development of and the imposition of the increasingly common top-down, political, bureaucratic, misguided school reform.

The new way to teach math. The newest way to teach writing. The revised testing process. The updated curriculum. The innovative school governance system. The latest matrix of numbers, factors, and assessments to provide a measure of school performance. A revision of the most recent revision to the testing process. Elimination of the writing method introduced three years ago to instead use another fleeting approach.

The inefficiency, the confusion, the wasted time, the wasted money, the damage done, the unintended negative impact, the counterproductivity of typical top-down, political, bureaucratic schemes of education reform lead to one conclusion—those reforms need to be challenged, defeated, and stopped.

Teachers often perceive that their input is rarely sought or, if sought, is rarely taken seriously in the creation of solutions to the problems of education. The experience of many teachers will confirm that perception. A teacher might express the frustration of teachers: "Those politicians, those bureaucrats, those higher-up powerful school monarchs think they know it all. They should come teach my classes for one week, then they would know twice as much as they know now. Of course, they would never last one full week as a teacher."

What is a conscience-driven teacher to do amid the perpetual barrage of school reforms that do not work? As stated earlier, using proper protocol, express ideas to the people in authority. Also, comply with all legal mandates, but far surpass those regulated routines and trendy gimmicks. Do what is required, but in addition do what works to cause learning.

Conscientious teachers could keep notes about and records of all decisions or actions that the education empire and its emperors force on schools. These notes and records will accumulate over the years as failed reform efforts follow other failed reform efforts. Document the failures, and then when an old idea that failed years ago is suggested for another try, present your documentation to the decision makers. They might listen. They might realize the path to failure they are on.

Dr. Earl Reum taught generations of student leaders that "people support what they help create." Conscientious teachers can apply that wisdom. Team up with other conscientious teachers to create a teacher think tank in your school that actually promotes thinking. Invite everyone to meetings.

At the meetings, think collectively. This teacher think tank is not guided by the political agenda of wealthy people who use their think tanks to guide the elite media or the politically powerful to certain controlled conclusions. This think tank is an intellectual democracy where truth emerges when ideas collide.

From the teacher think tank discussions can come teaching ideas that colleagues share, borrow, combine, and apply. These ideas are not political, bureaucratic, or otherwise out of touch with reality. These ideas are of, by, and for the classroom reality and are created with classroom realists. These ideas are purpose driven, classroom driven, and conscience driven. These ideas are expressed voluntarily, are adopted voluntarily, and are implemented voluntarily.

At each teacher think tank meeting participants give updated reports of the classroom results obtained from the use of recently traded ideas or recent mutually created ideas. Improvements are identified. New ideas are created. Old, successful, proven ideas are remembered. From this think tank, from the ideas of this think tank, actions that cause learning will follow.

This teacher think tank needs no new laws, no new taxes, no new policies, no new regulations, and certainly no new school reform programs. This think tank relies on the sincere desire of conscientious teachers to continually improve in their work plus to improve in the quantity of and the quality of learning that they cause in their classrooms.

Conscientious teachers challenge education reform because the typical reform is so disruptive, so frustrating, and so harmful. Laws, policies, and regulations must be obeyed; however, they are not the parts that define the wholeness of teaching.

Teachers know what works. Conscience-driven teachers do what works. When education reform forces a teacher to do what does not work, the teacher properly expresses concerns yet professionally complies; however, this honorable teacher also complies with the higher requirements of integrity, virtue, and duty.

Education reform may aggravate, dismay, annoy, bother, and irritate conscientious teachers, but education reform does not define, limit, or defeat those teachers.

Education reform movements will challenge your endurance, your attitude, and your energy. Respond by challenging education reform, outsmarting education reform, and by causing learning that is much more than and that is much better than any result that typical education reform efforts can achieve. Guided by the conscience of a teacher, you, as a conscience-driven teacher, can be the education reform that political, bureaucratic, top-down procedures can never be.

Chapter Seven

Communicate with Teachers

The teacher think tank idea suggested in chapter 6 is an example of teachers communicating with teachers. The results of such teacher-to-teacher shared, collaborative, and collective thinking can be quite favorable. How much teacher-to-teacher communication with depth and substance occurs daily? A minimal amount, because each teacher spends almost all of his or her time at school as the only adult in a classroom.

Teachers may talk briefly as they wait in line to use a copy machine, as they eat a hurried lunch in the faculty workroom, as they see a colleague who has hall duty in the morning before classes start, as they encounter each other in the faculty mailroom or in the school's office. Teachers spend the vast majority of their time working independently in their classrooms.

There are successes in classrooms each day throughout a school. There are difficulties in classrooms each day throughout a school. Some successful practices could be applied toward the difficult circumstances if teachers communicated more with each other about what is working well and what is not working at all, about what improvements some students made recently and what caused those changes, about students whose grades are improving and the ideas teachers created together to produce the improvements.

In the hurried busyness of a typical day at school, teachers have classes to teach, tests to type, copies to make, computer work to do so records are current, quizzes to grade using a machine at school, papers to grade using a pen plus using a teacher's judgment, a meeting to attend, a classroom to prepare for the instructional activities of the day, hallway supervision, emails to answer, knocks on the door, public address system interruptions during class time, phone calls about a student who must report to the office to pick up her lunch, and the unfortunate exit of all students from a classroom because of some pay-for-the-performance guest speaker whose promotional brochure convinced the principal to schedule this show to score some political-correctness points.

Amid such demands on the time and energy of a teacher, where are the opportunities to communicate with colleagues? Those opportunities must be created. Take the initiative to begin conversations with colleagues. Ask other teachers how they solve specific problems that you are facing. Ask other teachers how they work with students who misbehave in your classroom and whose schoolwork in your classroom is inadequate. Ask other teachers what works with their gifted and talented students to provide the proper instruction that nurtures their abilities.

Take the initiative by sending emails to colleagues, attaching a copy of a very successful homework project assignment that your students recently completed. This action could help establish a practice at your school of teachers submitting electronic copies of quizzes, tests, projects, homework assignments, and other instructional materials to a commonly accessible electronic idea bank to which every teacher can make a deposit and from which every teacher can make a withdrawal.

Do not stop with an electronic idea bank, however beneficial it can be. Involve yourself in interpersonal discussions that deal with enhancing academic instruction. The electronic idea bank provides a way to display ideas. Interpersonal discussions provide a process through which one idea interacting with another idea can create a third hybrid idea that surpasses the original two concepts.

The most effective teachers are not concerned about being the source of an idea but are concerned about obtaining and implementing the best ideas that cause the most learning and the highest quality learning. These teachers communicate with colleagues, read professional journals about the most effective ways to teach, read books about high-impact teaching, and continue to learn about the subject(s) they teach and the ways to teach that subject to their students to get superior results.

Proper communication among teachers excludes schoolhouse gossip, personal criticism of colleagues, unprofessional comments about students, and aimless complaints. Genuine concerns about students can be addressed properly so the real problem is correctly resolved. Gossip is wrong. What one teacher perceives to be questionable about another teacher is beyond the authority of and the full knowledge of the teacher whose perception is incomplete. Valid, 100 percent certain concerns can be reported to the school authorities, but that is the opposite of gossip.

"This place is awful. What's wrong with the principal? Does anyone ever see him? Does he ever leave his office? What about the assistant principal? She supposedly evaluated me last year, but all she did was stop by one time for fifteen minutes and then gave me some official form to sign saying I met all requirements. That was so phony. I got no guidance from that. And can you believe the person the principal hired to be the basketball coach? She's the daughter of the last superintendent. That superintendent hired our principal. I bet they set up that deal. Plus she has a so-called teaching job but it's only to check data on students all day and keep reports about them. What kind of a scam is that?"

School administrators need to communicate clearly, sincerely, and often with teachers. To the extent that professional confidentiality permits, a school administrator can explain decisions so that people at school understand what is being done, why those actions are being taken, and, when possible, how input can be received during the decision-making process.

Some decisions made by school administrators, especially those involving intricate personnel matters, are made behind closed doors and should be confidential. Other decisions made by school administrators can and should follow an open flow of or exchange of ideas, opinions, and concerns. When school administrators thoroughly communicate with teachers, it helps build a sense of working together. The absence of thorough communication creates a workplace atmosphere of suspicion, distrust, animosity, and resentment.

Conscientious teachers professionally communicate with students, with other teachers, with school administrators, with staff members at school, with parents/guardians of students, and with people in the education hierarchy. These teachers understand that such communication is part of the overall process that causes learning. These teachers know that they expect the teachers of their children to provide abundant communication.

For people who seek to impact schools through new laws, new regulations, new policies, new school reforms, or other initiatives, please do yourselves a big favor. Talk to and truly listen to many teachers before you take any action. Apply the ideas you get from teachers into any proposals you make. Listen closely to teachers throughout each step of creating a proposal, getting approval of the proposal, and while implementing the proposal. Communicate with teachers so that your ideas are based on the current classroom reality; otherwise your ideas will fail.

The conscience of a teacher is offended when teachers are not listened to, when school administrators or other school officials do not communicate with teachers, when school administrators create an inner circle of most favored people who get the best of everything at school because they are friends, and when employees who obviously are inept are still employed and are sometimes promoted. Please note, communication is not achieved with repetitive email blasts no matter how long, detailed, or graphically enhanced.

For many matters such as those, an individual teacher can have little or no impact. In the areas over which a teacher does have authority or control, exemplary work can be displayed. Inept or mediocre school administrators or education officials may not recognize the merit of exemplary work because they function in a world of cutting corners, making deals, covering their tracks, complying minimally with legalities, and staying in power. It is sad that education is wounded by and sabotaged by those evil forces.

In such political battles or turf wars, proceed with caution if at all. Communicate with wise, experienced, trustworthy colleagues when you, as one conscientious David of a teacher, consider taking on the politically powerful and good-old-boy/-girl Goliath network of unofficial alliances. Some battles must await another day or must be fought by someone else.

Deciding what battles to fight requires a conscience-driven teacher to honestly communicate with himself or herself. The conclusion could be "What is occurring here is wrong. Perhaps our teacher's organization in this school district can work on that. Alone, on this matter in this political reality, I would get nowhere. Still, I can and will cause learning each day in my classroom. And if I ever become a school administrator, I will never do that job the way I see it being done now."

A conscientious teacher cannot save the world and cannot save the universe of education, but can and must cause learning continuously in the classroom. The world and the education universe will benefit from that honorable work. Most of all, students will benefit from that exemplary work. With that achieved, the conscience of a teacher can have some peace.

Chapter Eight

Communicate with Administrators

"What do they do all day?" is a question commonly asked by teachers about school administrators. Specific versions of that question could inquire about "What does the principal do all day?," "What does the assistant principal do all day?," "What does the superintendent do all day?," "What do those people in the school district central office do all day?," and "How about the people at the state department of education? What do they do all day?"

Teachers know what they themselves do each day in their classrooms. Teachers lead instructional activities, check attendance, ask questions, respond to knocks on the door, correct misbehavior by students, collect homework, return graded tests, get pencils for students who never bring supplies to class, answer the phone when someone in the school office needs something, watch for cheating during a quiz, call on students during class discussions, deal with a student who is obsessed with his cell phone and who violates all rules about cell phones at school, moves around the room to see that all students are writing their one-paragraph reply to the opening question of the day, responds to the attendance clerk's public address system call to the classroom for a student who is leaving early, acknowledges the excellent answers given by students during the class discussion, takes a student into the hall for a quick conference about why she has to sit up and stay awake during class, and much more.

Teachers know the classroom activities of teachers and that they have more work than they have time during a day. Administrators have a secretary or two, may have an administrative assistant, and have some meetings that take them away from school. Teachers are independent, sole proprietors who have no secretary despite having much secretarial work to do, who have no support staff reporting directly to them, and are at school all day every day.

A conscientious teacher can learn more about what school administrators do and can offer to be of service when a committee set up by a principal needs a member or when an administrator asks for faculty volunteers for a new project. The classroom world of a teacher and the managerial world of a school administrator may seem to barely overlap, but neither should work in isolation when symbiosis is possible.

School principals and assistant principals get limited information about what happens in classrooms. Teachers are uniquely positioned to fill that communication gap. Inform the principal and the assistant principal(s) about projects, activities, instructional events, test or quiz results. Give them a copy of various assignments your students are doing. Invite them to class as a participant in instructional activities that apply to their career experience and that can enhance their favorable interaction opportunities with students.

People who work at a school district's central office may rarely spend time in classrooms, although some of those officials make more of an effort than others do to be in schools and to be in classrooms. Assuming no protocols prohibit this, occasionally inform district officials of work that you and your students are doing.

Some of those officials will appreciate the classroom view, while others may see one more email as a nuisance even though the email topics are teaching, learning, and students. Do not expect universal admiration and regard for your communication efforts, but know that the recipients of the classroom insights you share with them need to know what is occurring in classrooms, whether they welcome it or not.

Some school administrators and some school district officials are highly competent, deeply devoted to their work, are very skilled, and inspire greatness by their example.

Some other principals, assistant principals, or school district officials are mediocre at best and inept at worst. How did they get selected for the position they have? What favor was being returned when they were hired? What strange motives led a decision maker to select a less capable candidate instead of the most capable candidate for a school administration duty?

All school administrators, from the most capable to the utterly incompetent, need to be informed about instructional activity in the classrooms. Some school administrators make the effort to very vibrantly interact with students, teachers, and staff throughout the school with the highest priority being to spend time in classrooms. Other school administrators isolate themselves in their office, spending more time with a computer than with people.

Unless a teacher is told otherwise—it is important to not be insubordinate—keep the school administrators informed about what you and your students are doing. Those school leaders or misleaders, managers or mismanagers, need to know the classroom reality. It is common to criticize school administrators for reasons as varied as "Why don't they ever get out of the office?" to "They never listen to me" to "They just take care of their good friends. This place is so corrupt and dysfunctional."

Depending on the administrator, such criticism could be completely inaccurate, partially accurate, or completely accurate. Before being critical of school administrators, a conscientious teacher can learn more about what school administrators do.

Some school administration work is stealthy. What teachers do in the classroom is very visible and very observable. For administrators, some of their work is much less visible. The meetings attended, the paperwork done, the computer tasks that never end, the walk-in complainers who arrive in the office demanding to see the principal, the personnel matters to resolve, and other managerial tasks can absorb a school administrator's time and can take school administrators out of circulation from a school's hallways, classrooms, library, computer lab, cafeteria, and other school building areas.

Conscientious teachers can help administrators learn more about what is occurring in classrooms. Yes, school administrators should frequently visit classrooms for substantial observations and for active involvement in instruction. Realistically, that may not happen very much, but when being in the classroom often just does not occur for a school administrator, being informed often about what is taking place in classrooms can be done for administrators by teachers who conscientiously make that extra effort.

Do not send the principal an hourly update or a daily report. Inform the school administrators of the most important instructional activities, the best student work, the great improvement by a student, the superior test results. Also, ask for ideas when an instructional activity just did not work as you had hoped. This gives the school administrator an opportunity to be an instructional leader, which is part of his or her job description but which happens less than it is supposed to.

Let's assume that most school administrators have many items on their daily to-do list, plus they have endless situations that arise each day demanding immediate attention. Let's also assume that most school administrators sincerely care about education and are not concentrating on amassing power, tolerating the years until retirement, or merely avoiding getting fired.

The capable, caring, conscientious school administrators may deeply desire to be more of an instructional leader, but each day with its increasing complexity of new systems to implement, new reports to complete, more meetings to attend, and incessant emails to acknowledge, they find that their work is crisis management instead of being the teacher of teachers. Such managers and leaders deserve encouragement, help, and support. Being a conscience-driven teacher who keeps the principal informed means your classroom is a place the principal knows is a dynamic location where learning is caused.

Keep the principal and other school administrators informed of the achievements that occur in your classroom. They need to be reminded that amid the constant demands on their time, energy, priorities, work, career, and authority, they can always take a pause from unexpected management menaces and exhausting labors of leadership to once again be an educator. A conscientious teacher could be the person who helps a school administrator rekindle the hope that being a school leader could be done with the same heart, soul, drive, purpose, and convictions that led him or her originally to be a teacher.

The conscientiousness of a teacher can inspire a willing school administrator to increase or to recapture his or her original conscience-driven guidance and inspiration. The conscience of a teacher can graciously, caringly, and without seeking attention strengthen the resolve, cleanse the motives, improve the methods, and ignite or reignite the conscience of a school administrator. What a lovely thought. What a wholesome action. What a valuable and needed example.

Chapter Nine

Keeping Promises

As with school administrators—a group within which a wide range is found in terms of competence, commitment, people skills, management ability, leadership ability, and conscientiousness—there is a wide range among teachers in terms of competence, commitment, and conscientiousness. Can that range be experienced by one teacher during a career? Can an individual teacher have years of greatness, years of good work, times of ordinary work, and other times of low-quality work? The answer is yes. A resulting question is why. Another question is what needs to be done about these erratic results.

What does it mean when there is variation in work results from the same teacher throughout that teacher's career? What is revealed when a superior teacher becomes an average teacher, perhaps during part of a school year or perhaps for an entire school year or longer? How can that teacher recapture the greatness that once defined his or her classroom results?

What could cause scattered, irregular, uneven, and unsteady results? What events or factors take a teacher from the level of highly accomplished to ordinary to below average? What can take a teacher back to the highly effective level? Can this individualized variance be predicted, prevented, diagnosed, and corrected?

A conscience-driven teacher should be the first person to notice that his or her work performance has declined. A comprehensive self-evaluation could be very revealing. Honestly answering questions such as the following may help identify the forces working against the teacher. Some of the forces may be completely due to what the teacher is doing or not doing. Some of the reasons may be due to circumstances being imposed on the teacher by the school, the school district, the state government, or the national government. Life has its changes, its ups and downs unrelated to career, yet which can collide with work performance. Ponder the following.

1. Have I made changes in the instructional activities that I have designed for my students? If yes, what justified the changes? Have I identified more effective ways to teach, and have I begun using those improvements, or have I found simpler, less time-consuming, less energy-consuming tasks that occupy the students but do not fully teach the students?
2. Am I physically healthy? Is an unknown illness or health condition limiting what I can do? Am I taking good care of my physical health?
3. How frustrated and discouraged am I letting things at school make me? All of these silly changes we have to make will never work, but nobody listens. I have so much real work to do, so how can I obey the dumb directives forced on us? I know how to teach. Leave me alone. Am I the only person who feels this way? Could something be done to avoid more of these miserable mandates? Is everyone frustrated and discouraged?
4. Could I get some trusted colleagues to come observe me and help me figure out what is going on? Am I doing something wrong that I just am not realizing? Could I watch other teachers and get ideas from them?
5. Some of my students this year are incorrigible. No matter what I do, they misbehave; they disrupt class. I'm taking all of that very personally. It gets me down. The discipline system at this school has become so weak. Some students think they can get away with anything. I never let these things bother me so much before. I dealt with them and moved on. Why do I let the few students who cause trouble keep me from concentrating on all of the other cooperative students?
6. Things just are not like they used to be. Everything I learned in college and in graduate school about teaching has been replaced with lots of innovations. Why am I so opposed to these changes? Because I think they are no good, but those changes are the law now. Teaching now is not what teaching used to be. Should I change careers? Is that possible at this point in my life?
7. Maybe I underestimated some things. When I moved from an apartment to owning a house recently, I thought it would be great. It is a constant pain. Something always has to be fixed. I'm at school all day. How can I get repair people to fix my house when I'm teaching all day? Should I sell the house?
8. How annoyed am I that I have never been interviewed for any of the fourteen positions I applied for in this school district during the past three years? Academic dean, instructional coach, assistant principal, school counselor, and some others. I can do all of those. I'm better qualified than almost all of the people who got selected for those

positions. Why should I keep trying so hard and working so hard if nobody notices and if it never leads to anything?

9. Why can't I use some of the good-old-fashioned teaching techniques that always work? I assigned my eighth-graders the Gettysburg Address to memorize. Years ago I memorized that brilliant speech in the eighth grade. I still remember it. I was so proud when I recited it in class. The principal told me to cancel the assignment because some parents called to say their eighth-grade children were too stressed about this. Have we lowered the standards that much? Then the principal said to me, "They can get the Gettysburg Address on the Internet. No need to memorize it now." What is she thinking? The idea of memorizing it is not to access it only, but to know it, to understand it, to really appreciate it, and to exercise your brain in ways that an electronic screen cannot substitute for. What are schools becoming?

10. Am I as enthusiastic as I once was? Am I teaching my students with the energy and determination I had earlier in my career? Have I become a bit lazy? Am I cutting corners? Have I developed some bad habits?

11. Am I keeping all of the promises I made to myself when I selected teaching as my profession and when teaching chose me to lead a classroom? Have I let the passage of time, the changes in school, and some things in my life outside of school keep me from honoring those fundamental promises I made to myself deep within my heart, mind, and conscience?

12. What must I do to be great again as a teacher? What must I then do to stay great as a teacher?

13. What battles in education can I fight and win? What battles in education must I leave for others to resolve?

14. How determined am I to be great again as a teacher? Am I willing to do whatever it takes?

15. Whose advice and counsel should I seek? Whose thoughts should I avoid so they do not mislead me?

Conscientious teachers give abundantly of their time, effort, compassion, energy, persistence, endurance, heart, and mind. The results can be meaningful, gratifying, and heartening. Getting to those splendid results can deplete the human inner resources of any teacher. Those resources need to be restored.

A conscience-driven teacher may be inclined to make everything in education perfect. No one teacher can achieve that lofty, elusive goal. The exhaustion of mind, body, and soul that comes from the pursuit of the impossible denies the attainment of the possible. Set and pursue high, attainable results that cause improvement in students and in your teaching, but do not hold yourself responsible for the impossible.

Once today's possible is reached, a new level of possible can be sought tomorrow. Until then, pause, relax, rest, do something other than grade papers and prepare lessons. Among the promises that conscience-driven teachers must keep is the promise to take proper care of themselves. That will enhance your teaching. That will enhance your life.

Look at yourself in the mirror. Be honest. Look into your heart and soul, your mind and conscience. Be good to yourself by keeping the promises you once made to be a great teacher always. Also, make and keep the promise to take very good care of yourself.

For a conscience-driven teacher, one fundamental promise guides the classroom work more than anything else. "I promise to teach my students as I expect my own children to be taught by their teachers." Imagine the revolutionary results that can occur when that promise is the driving force in classrooms.

Chapter Ten

Self-Honesty

"I really don't know what happened. I mean, something went wrong. Something changed. I really did not notice much of anything at first, but then it got worse."

"When I came back to school in August it was about two weeks or so until the students would return for classes. We weren't at the point yet when teachers had to be at school, but I always come back several days early to get perfectly prepared for the start of the school year."

"I checked on school email from home occasionally during the summer, but it had been maybe three weeks since I had checked it. So there are eighty-four emails waiting for me. A lot of it was junk I could just delete, but about ten were from our principal explaining new stuff we had to do. There were ten more from our school district telling us, ordering us, to do more stuff. I came in to get some real work done to prepare for teaching, but it would take two days or more to finish some of the email requirements."

"What choice did I have? There were eight hours of online video training each teacher had to watch. You could not fast forward. There was a quiz every fifteen minutes or so to make sure we were paying attention. So I watched four hours of video material about the new teacher evaluation system. I'm not kidding, you could summarize the important parts in fifteen minutes."

"The video had a state government education leader reading a script telling us how to teach. I wondered if she had ever been a teacher. Then there were all of these short video segments showing examples of the way we are supposed to teach. They were awful. I would be embarrassed to use the simplistic stuff from those examples."

"Then there were online videos to watch for training about workplace safety. We watch these every year. More quizzes to take every fifteen minutes. The content is about like what children are shown to help them learn to look both ways at an intersection before they cross the street. I guess these videos satisfy some law or some insurance requirement. So I watched two hours of these. A ten-minute summary would have been plenty."

"Watching endless hours of video material is not the best way to teach. Why is that the way our school district does this training each year? No serious teacher would teach that way, but it's what we have to go through. It's a bad example. The school district does not do in its training program what it tells us we have to do with our teaching."

"The other two hours of online training was about Internet safety and technology protocols. We already know this. The online video is five or six years old. We watch it each year. They change the quizzes in it so we'll pay attention. This one needed five minutes to say all that was important, but it went on for two hours."

"I spent an entire day in my classroom finishing the video training. Another email said all teachers had to attend a training session either the next day or a week later. So, the next day, instead of doing what I needed to so everything would be ready for my students, I had to attend eight hours of a training session at school. We had our choice of going now, going in one week, or going on four school days after school for two hours each time. I just wanted to get it over with."

"The training was about a new plan our school district suddenly came up with to teach math across the curriculum. No matter what subject you teach or what grade you teach, math has to be included every day in every class. If you teach English, U.S. history, art, or any other subject, you must include at least five minutes of math calculation, math reasoning, math analysis, or math application."

"That is a really bad idea. Math teachers should teach math. They know math. They know how to teach math. Our school district says the math scores on state tests are low, so something has to be done. Here's my prediction. Math scores may increase, but other scores will go down because extra time on math means less time on everything else."

"I did my best to start the first day of the school year positive, but it was not easy. Budget cuts in our school district meant fewer teachers, and that meant class sizes were larger. Most years I had twenty-five, twenty-six, or twenty-seven students in my seventh-grade English classes. This year I had thirty, thirty-one, or thirty-two students in each class. Last year I had 156 students in my six classes. This year the number is 186. How would you like an increase in your workload of 19 percent?"

"During the year we had to document how we were including math in each lesson. We had to send a one-page electronic checklist, form, and description. That took fifteen minutes each day. And we had to attend two after-school sessions each month to get more information about math across the curriculum. More forms and more meetings on top of more students with more papers to grade and everything else."

"I'm not proud of this, but for the first time in my career I started calling in sick when I wasn't sick. I'd stay home one day every two or three weeks to grade papers for the entire day. I left plans for the substitute to show a video about a book or a story we were reading and, of course, to do five minutes of math."

"By the second semester I was sick, but not in a cough, cold, flu, illness way. I was sick of all the dumb stuff we had to do that year that was keeping me from teaching. I started talking to other teachers. Most of them agreed with me. One teacher said she had planned to teach for two more years, but she changed her mind and is going to retire at the end of this year. She said it just wasn't worth the fight anymore."

"That got my attention. So I talked to that teacher a lot. Janet is her name. I've known her for a long time. We've both taught here for years. I've been here ten years and she's been here much longer, maybe twenty-seven or twenty-eight years. What she told me really made me think."

"She said things had been changing for her during the past few years. Teaching just wasn't like it used to be. Two years ago she was observed five times by the principal. Usually the school administrators observe two or three times and then write up a pretty generic report making a few good comments or checking a list that says the teacher's work was acceptable."

"Well, the principal was in his first year as a principal and he must have wanted to show how powerful he was. He gave her an overall rating of below average and put her on a corrective action plan. She filed a grievance and won, so another person observed her the next year and that time her evaluation was outstanding. The principal never spoke to her again. He changed her teaching assignment from eighth-grade English to sixth-grade social studies, which she had not taught for twenty years. He had the authority to take that action. It was unfair. She did the best she could, but it was a difficult year."

"She was very honest with herself and realized that she could be a great sixth-grade social studies teacher, but it would take more time and effort than she could come up with after twenty-seven or twenty-eight years of teaching, plus her health had declined. She decided that the only honest action to take was to retire."

"She loves retirement. She works part time at a nursing home as the assistant activities director. She volunteers at the public library with an elementary school literacy partnership program. She realized when the time to retire from teaching had come. She said it was important to know when to retire. She meant that if a teacher stays too long and for whatever reason the work is just not going like it should, it would be bad for everyone."

"I'm nowhere near retirement, but when I am most honest with myself I seriously wonder if I can do this work for twenty more years. I've thought about that a lot recently. These changes at school are so wrong. I liked the way I taught during the first four or five years of my career. My students really worked and they learned. Then all of these new changes got forced on us."

"For the past five years there have been more dumb changes we have been told to do. It's like somebody wants to make teaching into assembly line work and teachers just add another exact part to the machine as it is manufactured."

"Come on. Students are not machines being assembled. Schools are not factories. Teaching is not assembly line work. Schools are people places, at least they should be and they used to be. If this stuff continues, what's the point of being a teacher? I got into this work to make a big difference in the education of my students, not to just read a script each day and do generic, prescribed, or prefabricated lessons."

"My best friend owns a very successful ladies clothing store. Her assistant manager recently left to take another job. My friend has asked me to consider becoming the new assistant manager. With school out for the summer, I'm going to work there for a month and see what I think. It could be my only chance ever to change careers. To be honest, it looks very attractive. It would break my heart to give up on teaching, but what I am doing now is not real teaching. It's following the daily chart telling us what to do and how to do it. I think it is going to get worse and teachers will be told everything to do. Our professional judgment won't matter. Our knowledge of teaching won't matter. We'll be robots doing what the school czar demands. Why would anyone with a sense of right and wrong belittle themselves by giving into that system?"

"If only I could be allowed to be a genuine teacher like I was allowed to at the start of my career. I'm afraid those days are over. I'm afraid I may need to leave before I'm stuck with no other career options."

"But first I'll talk to some people. I know a few teachers who quit teaching after several years in the classroom. They had different reasons, but I could find out how the career changes worked out for them. There's one teacher at this school who quit teaching once, but then came back and has been teaching ever since. I wonder why he came back. I'll get his advice too."

"I guess I could talk to some retired teachers and see what kept them going for all the years they taught. There must have been some difficult times, but they never gave up. I need to hear what they can tell me. It's time for some discussions I never thought would be necessary, but now is the time. This is too important for me just to think it through alone."

"Maybe I could take a year of absence and work in the clothing shop to see if that is a better career for me, but I could return if it did not work out. I don't know if that is possible, but I can find out."

"I never thought a career could get so complicated, but something is wrong and I can't deny it. I'm not the first person to be in this situation. Maybe other teachers here are feeling the way I am. There's no reason to be frustrated all alone. Somebody has words of wisdom for me. With the right advice this can be figured out."

Self-honesty for a conscience-driven teacher leads to a sincere evaluation of how well the teacher is doing his or her work. Self-honesty for a conscientious teacher also requires a genuine appraisal of the working conditions. Can I still do this job at this school as I expect it to be done? Can this job at this school still be done the way it should be?

The conscience of a teacher does not obsessively dwell on or exaggerate temporary troubles; rather, the emphasis is on what matters most and what works best. The difficulties of teaching are increasing in number and in severity, yet some teachers continue to thrive. What do they know? What do they believe? What are they doing to master the difficulties? Do they ever have doubts?

Those questions have answers that are obtainable when conscience-driven teachers are asked. When teaching is not going as it ideally should, when career satisfaction of earlier years has faded, when work is much more frustration and disappointment than it is productive and meaningful, self-honesty obligates the conscientious teacher to examine his or her essence and to find true answers to vital questions.

Be honest with yourself. Be gentle, be kind, be direct, be frank, be open to truth, beware of deception. Give yourself the gift of self-honesty. That will better enable you to give the gift of the best work you can do to the people you work with, the people you work for, the people you serve, and the service you provide.

The penetrating power of honesty is matched by the healing revelations of honesty. Conscience and honesty are best friends, teammates, and they are symbiotic. The conscience needs honesty. Honesty strengthens the conscience. Implement self-honesty now and always.

Chapter Eleven

Pure Law

The laws that govern public education must be obeyed. Some of those laws are beneficial, other laws do no harm, while others are harmful. Nonetheless, the laws must be followed; however, the harmful laws need to be challenged and changed or eliminated.

Policies and regulations that are legitimate actions of government agencies such as a state department of education or a local school board must be obeyed. Laws, policies, and regulations are products of the political process. Learning is the result of an effective teaching process. Those two processes are vastly different, which helps explain why some laws, policies, and regulations that apply to education are harmful to schools.

The work of lawmakers, policy writers, and regulation writers would be much more beneficial for education if the people who produce those directives intently listened to educators, especially teachers and also school building administrators. For educators to be heard they must speak up in the right way, at the right time, at the right place. What should guide the input from teachers who are conscience driven?

The answer is pure law. Pure law is not produced by the political lawmaking process. Pure law emerges from honor, virtue, integrity, honesty, and conscience. Pure law is not the result of compromise as political law is. Pure law is the result of a search for and a knowledge of rightness, ethics, what works best, and what matters most. Consider the following account.

Martha: I know that our school's administrative team persuaded the school council to pass the policy that every class has a full-length final exam at the end of each semester. I always do that in December when we have final exam days at the end of the first semester. Grades are due in early January, so there is plenty of time. I never do that in May at the end of the second semester. Who has the time? Grades are due instantly. I just give them a short set of multiple-choice questions and we call it a final exam. I don't see anything wrong with that.

Fran: My classes will have a full final exam next week to finish this semester just like we did in December. You're right about how busy everything gets in May, and we do have to turn in grades fast so the counselors can let any eighth-grader know if they are not passing for the year. Those students have to go to summer school if they want any chance of being in high school next year.

Martha: The students have chances all year long to do the work and pass their classes. Some of them do nothing on purpose and then do a little summer school work for a month in the summer. That's how they pass. I would take away that option. It just invites some students to cause trouble all year. About final exams: do eighth-graders really need those? What's the point?

Fran: I've always thought that the point is to give them a chance to think about everything they learned all year, especially this semester, and to put all of that together on one exam. The exams I give have three parts. There are fifty really complex multiple-choice questions that are not just remembering something but that apply what the students know. Then they have a short essay to write. The third part is something they draw, but the art quality is not emphasized. What's important is the thinking that goes into what they create and the ideas they communicate through the drawing.

The machine grades the multiple-choice part. I read the writing in about three or four minutes per student. The drawing can be rapidly graded with a quick, but serious, look at their creativity and the ideas they expressed. We have three days for the exams, so that's two classes per day. It makes for busy days, but I really like how much they have to think during the exam. I design the exam so they keep learning as they take the exam. Good exams are part of how I teach my students.

Martha: I still think it is too much to ask us to do at the end of the year. The principal and the assistant principal don't have any exams to grade, but they love to pile the work on us. They have never questioned what I do for my exam because technically it follows the exam policy. If they even seriously questioned me I can defend what I do and prove to anyone that I am not doing anything wrong. The way you do things is so much more work. You could do a lot less and not get in any trouble.

Fran: Oh, trouble is not my concern. I'm not interested in doing less. I had some teachers years ago in middle school that gave us the hardest final exams I had ever seen. They prepared us and I always did well, but those exams were rough. Then in high school when I had exams it was easy. I also had a few middle school teachers who gave us no exam at all. On exam days they told us to read and be quiet. I always promised myself that when I became a teacher I would be like my teachers who always had tough tests and hard exams. They did everything in their classes all year like that. I learned the most from them even if at the time I wished they would ease up.

Martha: You work too hard. Be careful or the principal might make all of us do exams your way.

Fran: My own children are in sixth and seventh grades now. I just ask myself if I am teaching my students the way I want my children to be taught. That's not a school policy; it's my policy. That's not a state law; it's my law. My policy requires more than what our school policy requires, and my law is better than the state laws on education. When I obey my policy and my law I more than obey what the school and the state insist on. I just try to concentrate purely on what I would want for my children, and then that's what I do for my students. The results are good, and I feel great about it.

Martha: Well, we both get good evaluations each year so I guess there are different ways of doing things. It's always good to visit at lunch. Time to go back to class. Have a great final exam this semester. See you at lunch tomorrow.

What motivates Fran to do much more than is required by the school's policy on final exams? What guides Fran to do more each day than would be required by policies, regulations, laws, or her employment contract?

Fran obeys a pure law, which is based on the standard that she will do as much for her students as she expects teachers to do for her children. She sets her standard as teaching her students with the quality of instruction that she would provide if her own children were in her classroom. Her devotion to students is exemplary. Her motive is honorable. Her inspiration is pure. The results are superior.

In the arena of education, politically made laws, regulations, and policies are necessary, but they are not the ultimate standard. They include a variety of motives, agendas, and goals, some of which are beneficial, some of which do no harm, some of which are harmful.

A conscientious teacher is obligated to obey laws, regulations, and policies. A conscientious teacher also goes far beyond mere completion of legal mandates because the conscience-driven teacher follows a pure law that allows only actions that are most beneficial. This pure law filters out actions that, while doing no harm, also do no good. This pure law filters out actions that are harmful.

Laws, regulations, policies, and contracts establish required levels of performance and mandated actions. Comply with them. Then rise above them by looking deep into your conscience and finding a pure law. Great teachers have always done that. It is not a secret or a mystery. It is a noble adventure into greatness.

There are groups that seek to impact education and whose motives lead them to create problems for schools, for school administrators, for teachers, and for students.

Think tanks create proposals that satisfy the financial sponsors of the think tank. Foundations provide funds for specific actions they support, and their money can be very tempting, even when what they promote is not what schools really need. Interest groups concerned about various topics can seek to promote their issues as decisions about schools are made.

Democracy properly permits all of these voices and other voices to be heard. The voices of conscientious teachers must be heard clearly, often, and effectively. Enforcing the pure law in your classroom is vital. Expressing the insights that are based on pure law to education decision makers can help inform them of what only conscientious teachers know about education. Be courageous. Be pure. Be heard. Be a great teacher. Enforce pure law.

The employment contract must be obeyed. That is a legal and professional obligation. The best teachers comply with the terms of their employment contract, yet they vastly surpass those terms.

Conscience-driven teachers comply with a contract, a vow, a covenant that is higher than, more bold than, more beneficial to students than the legal terms of the employment contract. These teachers abide by an unwritten, unspoken bond that is deep within and honorably between their heart, mind, and soul.

Conscience-driven teachers demonstrate an exemplary, complete compliance with their employment contract. Then they advance beyond that standard law language to obey the imperatives of pure law. The employment contract has an important function. Pure law has a vital, vibrant, life-changing function. It is not a question of selecting one or the other. It is a proper and magnificent opportunity to embrace both.

Chapter Twelve

Great Examples

In searching for the right way to teach, the most effective way to teach, the best way to teach, wisdom can be found in great examples from the most outstanding teachers.

Think of the best teacher you ever had. What did she do in the classroom that gives her the highest ranking? What did she not do that average or below-average teachers did? What inspired and what sustained your best teacher to provide you with a superior educational experience? Consider these reflections of teachers as they recall the best teacher they ever had.

CASE STUDY 1

"It's been years since I thought about Ms. Sommerton. She was my sixth-grade math teacher. I hated math. I hated sixth grade. I hated middle school. She made it very clear that she loved everything about math and about sixth grade. She was so enthusiastic and excited."

"I started to wonder why Ms. Sommerton was so energetic in our math class. She talked about numbers and word problems and even fractions like all of those things were friends of hers. I had never seen a math teacher or any other teacher show so much exuberance every day. No matter what the exact topic in math class was on any day, Ms. Sommerton seemed to think it was the most important thing in the world."

"She had this way of making math seem as if it was actually important in real life. She spent time finding out what we were interested in. For me, when I was twelve years old nothing mattered more than saving money because my parents said I could get a very fancy new bicycle if I saved half of the money it would cost. Then they would pay the other half."

"Other students in the class had all kinds of interests like soccer, food, space travel, farming, swimming, archery, cooking, books, video games, horses, even the stock market. Day after day Ms. Sommerton had math problems for us to solve, but they weren't out of a textbook every day. She made up calculations about money, soccer, horses, space travel, and everything else we were interested in."

"Finally fractions made sense to me. I had never thought of money and fractions going together, but they do. I had to save $150. When I had saved $25 that was one-sixth of the money I needed. When I saved another $25 that would be two-sixths of the money, or I could call it one-third. I liked calling it one-third because it sounded more impressive, but I knew it was equal to two-sixths. When I got to $75 I was halfway to my goal. I suddenly loved math, even fractions, because it mattered to me. Sixth grade and middle school became fantastic because Ms. Sommerton showed me how what we do at school connected with my life."

"She even talked to some of my other teachers, and they used her idea. In science class I got to do a project about how money is manufactured at the mint and by printing. In history class I got to research about money from all kinds of civilizations and places. In English class I was allowed to read books that taught children how to manage money."

"I think often of Ms. Sommerton. Those are wonderful memories. I should do more with my students the way she did things with us. She made a big impact on me. She worked a lot harder than most teachers. She cared more, too. I think she was just that type of person. She cared about us so much and we could tell because of everything extra she did for us. She never had to say that she cared because she showed that she cared. That is an outstanding example to follow."

CASE STUDY 2

"My approach to this question has two parts. First, I'll tell you about my worst teachers. I will not mention names, but I will tell stories about a few people in particular. I'll create a group picture of my worst teachers and tell you about them so you see them as a group."

"They were awful, just awful. One was a high school football assistant coach. All he ever did was give us worksheets to do in class while he sat at his desk and worked on plays and practice drills or analyzed statistics from the most recent game. He had a student aide each class period. That student graded our worksheets. As I recall, this coach and his team won a lot of football games, but he never won anything in the classroom as a teacher."

"Another one of my worst teachers always did the same thing in our classes. We read each chapter out loud in class with one paragraph per student. Then we answered the questions at the end of the chapter. It never changed. We learned just about nothing."

"One other bad teacher tried hard. I mean she really worked, but everything was disorganized. We would start one activity and before finishing it we went to another activity. When papers were returned to us after she graded them there were always mistakes in what she had done. Everyone knew she got to school early every day, but nobody could figure out what she did with all of that extra time. It never was noticed in class."

"Those three teachers had a lot in common. They seemed distracted. They did not concentrate on whether we were learning. They just went through some motions of teaching, but it was not real teaching. It was fake. They didn't do themselves or us any good. I have wondered sometimes why they became teachers and why they were hired."

"Yes, I do remember my best teacher, Mr. Thomas Stevenson. He taught World History to me when I was a high school sophomore. He made us take notes his way with an exact system. He made us write long research papers. He called on every student in class each day. He gave us essay tests that challenged the smartest students. He loved World History, and he thought we should love it. I never was all that fond of World History, but I did the work and I sure learned. No class in high school was harder than World History with Mr. Stevenson."

"Back then I complained about having so much work for that one class, but I know it was helpful. He challenged us to be scholars. That was the word he used. I had never been challenged like that, but it worked. I decided that being a scholar was much better than being the typical, average student. That happened because Mr. Stevenson was no typical, average teacher."

CASE STUDY 3

"My best teacher was Ms. Grace Crawford. She was my third-grade reading teacher. Her classroom was all about reading. There were displays of books. There were shelves of books. There were pictures of authors. There were stories, biographies, fiction, nonfiction books, and more. You got the idea that Ms. Crawford lived with books."

"And she did. When we took time in class for everyone to read, Ms. Crawford sat in front of the room and read. When we presented book reports in class, Ms. Crawford also presented a report about the book she had just read. When we went to the library to check out a book, she talked to everyone individually to be sure we got a book that was good for us. Of course, she checked out a book and asked us for suggestions before she selected her book."

"I think what is most memorable is that she learned with us. She was certainly in charge of her no-nonsense classroom. We behaved and we worked or we were in trouble, but there was rarely any trouble. We had this kind of togetherness in the classroom. We were a community. It never felt like some classrooms where the students and the teacher are enemies. Ms. Crawford was the boss, but she was a respected boss. She understood us and took real interest in us. You could just tell how much it meant to her that we loved to read as much as she loved for us to read."

CASE STUDY 4

"I'll be honest. I don't have a best teacher from school. Our community was not known for the school system. Our schools were not terrible and our teachers were not incompetent, but our schools were ordinary and nobody complained that I can remember. It was all good enough for us."

"Now things at home with my mother were different. She was my best teacher. She gave me homework to do. I had to practice handwriting until it was perfectly clear. I had to memorize quotations, Bible verses, the multiplication table, the Gettysburg Address, foreign language words, and even the ancient Greek alphabet."

"My high school did not make us write research papers. My mother did. Every semester in high school I had a research paper assigned by my mother. These were long papers. She made me do endless hours of research using books and articles. She said computers might do the work and the thinking for me, so I had to use books and articles mostly. Anything I got from a computer I had to show her first and get her approval before I could use it."

"It's funny, but when I assign research projects to my students, they have to start with books and articles. We spend three days in the library for research, and they can't touch a computer until the third day. I see what books and articles they are reading, and I take notes. I insist that they use those print sources in their paper."

"Sure, they can use computer online sources, but if they started with the Internet they would never do anything else for the paper. Call me old-fashioned, but I know what works and I know that some of the old ways of teaching did not stop working just because something new came along."

Examples of great teaching are in the memories of most people who think thoroughly of their years as a student. Additional examples of great teaching can be found in schools today. Just ask people at a school and they can tell you who the best teachers are. Visit those teachers and learn from those teachers.

We know what works in teaching. Highly effective teachers past and present have not kept their methods, styles, or actions of superior teaching as secrets. Part of being a conscientious teacher is realizing that no one teacher knows everything, yet wisdom from many superior teachers can add up to a complete understanding of what the best teachers do to cause learning and how those best teachers do their work.

As the conscience of a teacher seeks eternal truths about teaching, part of the search is to obtain the insights and wisdom from great teachers of the past and of the present.

There are many complex systems and charts that claim to provide detailed descriptions and checklists of the characteristics of great teaching. These spreadsheets tend to be excessively wordy, complex, mechanical, impersonal, formula based, impractical, and bureaucratic. Based on research that has involved asking over four thousand educators to tell what their best teachers did, the characteristics of highly effective teachers include the following:

1. They use a variety of teaching methods and activities.
2. They challenge their students.
3. They are enthusiastic about teaching, students, and learning.
4. They make connections between what students need to learn and the wholesome knowledge, talents, and interests of students.
5. They work hard, they work smart, they get results.
6. They continuously learn more about what they teach and how to teach better.
7. They are not satisfied with anything less than the best work from their students and from themselves.
8. They sincerely and deeply care; they put that concern into action.
9. They do much more and much better than is required according to laws, policies, regulations, or an employment contract.
10. They are guided by ethics, honor, virtue, integrity, plus a standard of doing for their students what they would want teachers to do for their own children.

Great examples have been available always, and great examples from the present can be added to the vintage treasury. Conscience-driven teachers fully secure the gems that are the easily available insights from great examples of teaching. Conscientious teachers add, by their own work, more great examples to the certain body of knowledge about what works in classrooms to cause learning.

Chapter Thirteen

Real People

The conscience is not quantitative or statistical. Conscience-driven decisions are not numerical or data controlled. Virtue, honor, integrity, and conscientiousness are not measured by numbers.

Some numbers are useful in education. Grades are calculated. Attendance is measured. Test scores are analyzed. Budgets are mathematical statements of necessities, priorities, and affordable options. Salaries, wages, and benefits are expressed in amounts of dollars.

Data, numbers, and statistics do not reveal complete truth in education. Truth in schools comes from people and is about people. There is more to people than statistics can measure. There is more to learning than data can show. There is more to teaching than any quantitative analysis can indicate.

When the ideal teaching and the ideal learning occur there is an authenticity, a realness to the experience. Data cannot measure the presence or the absence of this real, authentic teaching and learning. The conscience of a teacher knows when the ideal teaching and the ideal learning happen. What does the conscience know that numbers cannot measure, that quantitative evaluation cannot identify, that statistical or data-driven prescriptions cannot fully formulate?

The conscience knows that students are real people living real lives right now. The conscience knows that teachers are real people, living real lives filled with many responsibilities right now, including to family, to career, to employer, to self, to friends, and to organizations.

The realness of the lives being lived right now by students and by teachers cannot be completely, accurately, or comprehensively measured by data. Of course, data can be useful. When a person's temperature is checked, a number tells if there is a fever; however, that one number does not fully describe how the person feels.

When a student takes four state-required annual tests in April or May, the data from those tests cannot provide a total description of what the student has or has not learned, has or has not achieved, has or has not experienced.

The totality of learning cannot be revealed by numbers alone. The totality of teaching cannot be described, measured, guided, evaluated, or defined by numbers alone.

Biographies are not filled with hundreds of pages of statistical charts. Biographies have few numbers; rather, those books explore events, decisions, trials and errors, challenges and successes, aspirations and ordeals, opportunities lost, lessons learned, and lessons ignored.

A student's educational biography is quite incomplete it if is merely a collection of data, numerical charts, and numbers. At least, insights about what the statistics mean are needed; however, insights that can come only from the narratives that spring from human interaction are more necessary.

Numbers, data, statistics can tell some parts of what happens in schools, but cannot tell, reveal, express, communicate, or describe everything that happens in schools. What can tell the full narrative, the fully human account of the totality of teaching and learning?

People can listen to people and interact with people. Numbers are one-dimensional. People are multidimensional. Charts filled with school data are finite. Learning is infinite. Conscientious teachers do not stop at the finite when the infinite is possible.

Education is not about data despite how useful numbers can be. Education is about people. Schools are ideally of, by, and for people, real people.

CASE STUDY 1

"Our department has been asked, actually told, to spend six hours of our professional development requirement analyzing data from the tests students took last May. We will meet to do this on Thursday, August 12. Teachers will return to school on Monday, August 16. If the August 12 schedule does not work for you, other options will be made available later for some professional development sessions to be held on several days after school dismisses for the day. Please respond to this email by Monday, August 9, so all plans can be made for our data analysis work."

In response to the above email, two teachers who saw each other at a local store where they were buying back-to-school supplies for their classrooms had this conversation.

Kim: Janet, how are you? How's summer been? Are you ready for school?

Janet: Kim. So good to see you. I thought I was ready for school until I read that email about the professional development day next Thursday that we have to attend. It sounds like a big waste of time to me. I've seen so many programs like this. It's always about the latest cure-all for schools. The current obsession is data. I've been a teacher for thirty-two years. We were not obsessed with data when I started, and we did a better job back then. The numbers can get in the way. Anyway, how are you?

Kim: I'm doing fine. I got engaged last week. I'm so excited.

Janet: What a beautiful ring. Oh, I'm so happy for you. I remember meeting your boyfriend. He's wonderful. When's the wedding?

Kim: At Christmas. We're both from here so we'll get married right here in our hometown. We go to the same church, so we have that reserved. There is so much to do. We are very excited.

Janet: Now tell me, did you say yes to him because of all the data analysis you did on the tests you had him take or were there other reasons? Did you have professional development about the data of getting engaged?

Kim: That's pretty funny, Janet. We did a lot of financial analysis, but numbers really had nothing to do with our decision to get married. We are devoted to each other. We've known each other since elementary school. We dated some in high school, but we went to different colleges. Then we both came back home after college, and we started dating each other again. So after three years of dating we are really ready to get married. Everything in me, everything I believe says this is right. He agrees, of course. His parents and my parents are thrilled. It's just what is meant to be. Getting married is so right for us.

Janet: Sorry to change the subject, but we can't escape that professional development that's coming up. Can you see anything good in it?

Kim: I'm finishing my master's degree during the next school year. I've had two courses in data and statistics for educators. It's all about analyzing test scores and stuff. I've been a teacher for only three years and I can see that what the big data is all about and the actual work we do with our students are miles apart, even worlds apart. I know my students. You know your students. A day of training on how to get students who never do any work to finally wake up and be responsible would help a lot more than what we'll have to sit through.

62   *Chapter 13*

Janet: It never changes. With all of the tests our students have to take for the state department of education, somebody wants to prove that the tests are useful, so they make us analyze the data and then report our findings and then somehow change our teaching because of the data. I get real data every day from the real work we do in my classroom. These other statistics are unreal.

Kim: You are right, but the people who run everything never listen to us. We have to do what they tell us. I think they forgot what it's like to teach. It's not about numbers. It is all about students and getting them to learn. Well, I need to finish getting these supplies. Let's send the data about what we're spending on our students to the school board. Think they will pay us back?

Janet: I doubt that is the type of data they care about. See you at school soon. Congratulations on your engagement. I am so happy for you.

It is 82 degrees outside, 90 percent humidity, gentle breeze, 40 percent chance of rain. Do those numbers fully describe the weather? No.

The stock market is up 0.7 percent, the unemployment rate is down 0.1 percent, corporate profits are up 4 percent for ten companies reporting today. Do those statistics fully describe the economy? Would volumes of data fully describe the economy? Could answers to questions asked of real people give uniquely insightful descriptions of the economy that numbers miss or incompletely analyze?

The weather impacts real people, and real people respond to the weather. The economy impacts real people, and real people react to, participate in, benefit from, or can be harmed by the economy. The weather and the economy cannot be described fully by numbers.

School is a people place. Teaching and learning are very much about people experiencing educational activities.

There are many numbers about schools, and some use of those numbers can be helpful. Still, schools are not about numbers and are not fully, accurately, or most significantly described by numbers.

Schools are about people. To know schools fully and correctly is to know the people at school, to know what occurs in classrooms at school, and to know everything else people at school do throughout their many school experiences.

School is about real people. Numbers are a tool to partly measure some aspects of school. Use the numbers to the extent that they are helpful. Do not be dominated by the numbers. Numbers do not have a conscience. You do have a conscience. Let the conscience lead and make the numbers follow. Do not let the numbers lead and make everyone and everything, conscience included, follow the dictates of data.

Chapter Fourteen

Know When

Perhaps when is now, right now. When may have been a few years ago. When could be a few years from now. There are different when moments. A conscientious teacher needs to know when.

Know when it is time to leave school and go home because other parts of your life need your time, effort, involvement, and presence.

Know when an unexpected learning opportunity has developed during a class, perhaps due to a question asked by one student, perhaps due to the reaction of the entire class to an historical photograph, perhaps due to how intellectually captivated students have become about a topic discussed in class. Quickly adjust the lesson and make the most of this unplanned learning celebration.

Know when it is time to respond to an email and when it is time for no response. One suggestion is if there is any doubt, do not respond. Give yourself more time to think, to reflect, and to consider what happens if you respond. When you do respond, be very selective, objective, and concise with what is communicated. Instant reactions can create enduring problems, so pause, think, edit.

Know when to speak at a meeting and know when to remain silent. Listen to your conscience, not to your ego. Abide by solid judgment, not by impulse or impetuous reaction. What is said cannot be unsaid. Select the times to speak, always speak wisely, and select the words to say cautiously.

Know when to refer a discipline matter to a school administrator. This action is not taken out of frustration or fatigue. This action is taken after the options you have as a teacher have, despite every reasonable and professional effort you can make, not corrected the student's continued disobedience.

Know when to contact a school administrator immediately about student misbehavior, including situations that pose real or potential threats to human safety and health. Ask school administrators to explain to the faculty what, based on their experience and training, should be communicated to them instantly.

Know when a student is being unreasonable, and do not respond in an unreasonable way. "Well, you're a terrible teacher" is not followed with an equally cruel comment; rather, respond neutrally. "Jason, the instruction you were given was to hand your cell phone to me because you were using it in class." "But that's not fair. I hate you." "Jason, the instruction you were given was to hand your cell phone to me because you were using it in class." Do not enter the trap that Jason is knowingly or unknowingly setting. Stay in control, and stay in self-control.

Know when to seek another position in school work. Being a school counselor, an assistant principal, a curriculum coach, or a school district official may appeal to you. Know why it is appealing and know what you would be getting into. Those duties are within the educational enterprise, but they are not in classrooms. Know also that other people will have the same ambition and that the most qualified person is not always selected. As is true in other organizations, friends may take care of friends, good-old-boys and -girls may protect others in the good-old-boy-and-girl network.

Know when to get help. There is no reason to teach in miserable isolation. There is no reason to let one defiant, disruptive, incorrigible student destroy class daily. There is no need to let your frustrations build to a personal crisis or to a career crisis. Get good advice from trusted colleagues. Get ideas and perspective from people who work outside of education. Rely on the guidance and support that can come only from family members.

Know when to offer help. As you talk to a first-year teacher about the disappointing and occasionally agonizing ordeals she is experiencing, the responses are not "It will get better" or "Hang in there" or "Have a good day." Be the person who truly listens, who offers real ideas, who consistently encourages, who keeps in touch, who shares instructional materials and activities that have worked for you, who remembers how very difficult the first year of teaching is and who offers the active concern that you wish someone had offered you years ago.

Know when it is time to retire. This is determined in part by age, by years of experience, by financial calculations, and by health conditions. Another pair of factors would be to listen to your mind as it tells you whether you can continue to do this work or not, and listen to your conscience as it tells you whether you should continue to do this work or not. Beware of the point of diminishing returns when the results you achieve are declining and when the satisfaction you obtain is declining. Both of those declines can be addressed and usually can be resolved, but there comes a time to declare victory and move on.

Know when the faculty workroom conversation has become unprofessional and redirect the discussion or just leave. Do not condone and do not be part of gossip, rumors, or any breach of confidentiality.

Know when questionable innovations in teaching and trendy, useless fads in education are not causing learning. If you are mandated to impose the faulty commands, then obey, yet add the instructional activities that your experience proves will work so that the desired learning goals are reached. In the right way and the right time, talk with teaching colleagues and school administrators about your concerns that the trends and the fads are false imitations of teaching, but know that trends and fads have supporters who may be powerful people.

Know when you have begun to make compromises that earlier in your career were quite unacceptable. "It's Friday. I'm really tired. I'll just get a video and my classes can watch it. This has been a busy week. It won't hurt to slow down for one day."

Then one occasional day for a video becomes one day each week for a video, and the compromise is no longer seen as a retreat from higher standards of superior teaching but has become a permanent lowering of standards. Know when the first thought of a compromise that is unprofessional begins to settle in your mind. "I can hear the classrooms near my room. Those people use videos all the time. Maybe I'm missing something. Maybe videos are better than I thought." Beware of being deluded, deceived, or tricked. Listen to the honesty from your conscience instead of the ill-advised illusions of instructional counterfeits.

Know when you need training in something and get that training. "The computer tells me that some of my students have complex medical issues. I need to know more than a medical alert icon on the computer screen tells me in case a real emergency arises." "I never studied special education, but I have to provide proper educational services. I need to be told how that is done." "I have some gifted and talented students, but nobody makes sure they get the learning experiences they need. It's up to me. I'm going to get trained in that."

Know when you have made a mistake. Correct the mistake. "I just realized that I did not enter grades for this class correctly on the test we had yesterday. I will correct that right after school today. The grade on the test paper you are getting back now is correct. By 4:00 this afternoon the computer grade information will match the score you are seeing now."

Know when you grade student work with a lower standard than you used earlier in your career or with a lower standard than your teachers used to grade your work. Telling students that their ordinary work is good or that their above-average work is great serves no valid purpose. Tell the truth and work with students so that they understand the truth, apply the truth, and make improvements.

Know when you have done all that one person can do and accept the peace that can come from giving yourself credit for accomplishing all that is possible. Do not hold yourself responsible for what no person or people can achieve. Is a dentist successful only when no patient ever has a cavity? Is a physician successful only when all patients are cured 100 percent? Are parents successful only when all of their children live flawless lives?

Know when you have done excellent work and commend yourself for that. Few other people will know of your outstanding effort and achievements. Fewer still will acknowledge your conscientious work. Be conscientious anyway because it is who you are, because it is ordained by your conscience, and because it is right.

Know when to calm down and walk away. There will be situations at school that accelerate your pulse. Some student misbehavior incidents can consume a teacher's energy, optimism, and endurance. Some unwise decisions made by school administrators can stir anger within a faculty. Some political or bureaucratic mistakes imposed on schools can enrage teachers. Being enraged is unhealthy and is unproductive. Give yourself some calm, tranquil, serene moments. Think, reflect, consider options, evaluate the impact of each option. Know when to act, but first know that some actions must await serenity.

What is your career telling you it is time for now? What is your daily work telling you it is time for now? What is your conscience telling you it is time for now? What "when moment" are you facing now? What "when moment" have you sought to avoid or delay but must deal with now?

Know when. Know that when could be now, at this moment, at this place. Life events are parts of knowing when. A career is important and deserves a high priority; however, a person is not defined or described fully by his or her career. Marriage, children, helping your parents as they age, dealing with the deaths of family and friends are among the life events that are higher priorities.

Give career the proper time, effort, and commitment it deserves, remembering that the conscience of a teacher is also the conscience of a person who is a spouse, who is a parent, who is an aging parent's vital advocate, and who is a source of comfort to family members or friends facing life's difficulties. Your conscience says to be an honorable, effective, superior teacher as part of being an honorable, caring, loving person.

Chapter Fifteen

Mandatory Teaching

A college sophomore sought advice from her aunt who had been a high school teacher for twenty-eight years. The college student, Katy, asked Aunt Judy a question filled with emotion, yearning, and a longing for certainty.

Katy: Aunt Judy, how did you know that you were supposed to be a teacher? You've told me that there were other options. The local newspaper knew you were a great writer for your college paper, and you had that job offer to be a reporter. One local television station saw the work you did as an intern there and said they would hire you. You majored in journalism and in English. Why become an English teacher instead of a journalist or something else?

Aunt Judy: I did like journalism a lot, and people told me I was good at it. I gave that career serious thought. It would have been a wonderful career and a good life. I think I could have become the editor of a newspaper or the general manager of a television station. But teaching had a grip on my heart. It may sound egotistical, but I thought I could do better teaching than a lot of my teachers did. It seemed wrong to me that some of my teachers just gave us worksheets to fill out or movies to watch. We would do those things while the teacher did something else. I had one teacher who would grade papers while we watched a movie. You always knew when she had a lot of papers to grade because we would have two or three days in a row of movies to watch. I had that one coach who was my ninth-grade science teacher. We had movies all the time. We never did an experiment or any real science. She spent all her time doing something with statistics and plays for her basketball team. I wondered then why she wasn't fired. Now I know. Some schools talk about teaching, but their real priority is sports.

So I got the idea that I could teach better than most of my teachers. I thought people who wrote for the local newspaper were better writers than I was. Same with television reporters. I wanted to do something I could be the best at. Actually, a school can have lots of great teachers. Nobody has to be the best, but I thought I could be a great teacher and only a good journalist.

And, it just felt different. I got much praise for the writing I did in college for the school newspaper, but I never thought what I wrote about was all that important. The school newspaper would have been fine without my articles. I never felt that way when I volunteered to work with the high school youth group at church while I was in college. I felt that it was important to be with them. I felt like I was supposed to be with them. I thought they needed me.

Katy: Is feeling something enough of a reason to become a teacher? How far will feelings get you when the work can be so tough and the students can act so bad?

Aunt Judy: You are right. It takes a lot more than a feeling. There have been many tough days and tough years in my career. Some students refuse to work and just never behave correctly. Other students are really scholarly and polite. I decided that both groups needed me. I also decided that I needed to be with students.

Katy: Did you ever think you had chosen the wrong career? Did you ever want to quit?

Aunt Judy: Yes to both questions. After my second year of teaching I did quit. Enough is enough. I spent fifty hours at school each week and twenty or twenty-five hours at home each week grading papers and preparing lessons. Nobody noticed and nobody cared. I did so much more than was required, and it was getting me nowhere. The principal of my school almost never left his office. He had some buddies who were employed as teachers at the school, but everyone knew they did nothing. I got out of there. I sold real estate for two years, and I was great at it. Seventy hours of real estate work each week put me in the top 10 percent of realtors in this city. I had a great future waiting for me in real estate, except there were no students among my clients. I missed teaching. Real estate could get along without me. I thought teaching needed me, and I realized that for better or worse, I needed teaching.

I decided that for me teaching was not just something I could do. Teaching was something I had to do. Teaching and I needed each other. It was mandatory for me to teach. Not to sound too philosophical, but it seemed to me that life itself was telling me to teach. I've been teaching for the past twenty-six years, so that's a total of twenty-eight years altogether as a teacher.

Katy: I know things in schools have changed a lot. I have already spent time in schools doing research for an introduction to teaching class I took this semester. The class is designed to help us decide if teaching is a good career choice. About half of the students in the class have decided no. It's good that they found out now instead of later when it would be too late to change their major and stuff. I've interviewed fifteen teachers. Most of them are glad to teach, but they all told me how much harder their work is every year. What kept you going after twenty-eight years of everything getting harder at school?

Aunt Judy: It is harder. There is so much nonsense we have to confront. To be honest, a lot of really stupid changes get forced on schools every year. But despite all of that I can still get a lot done with almost all of my students.

Katy: How much longer do you think you'll keep teaching?

Aunt Judy: Not much. Two more years of teaching is my plan. There's a reason to retire. At the end of my second year of teaching I was really frustrated because so much more could have been done and so much more should have been done. I left teaching after that, but I came back with a different frame of mind. I would do my very best every day. I would maintain the highest possible work ethic. I would challenge myself and my students. Nothing less than our best would be acceptable. I think I've lived up to that way of thinking and way of working. But I also think it is soon going to be the time when all the years of being a soldier in the classroom will have taken a toll. I want to retire while I'm still doing great work. I do not want to linger for years after I have begun to decline.

I intend to keep working after I retire. I really hope to work part time then for your university. My goal is to work with the college students who are student teaching and then to be the university contact person on those support committees schools have for first-year teachers. I hope to help the next generation of teachers after I move out of the way so one of them can take my place in the classroom.

Katy: One more question. When everything goes wrong, what keeps you going?

Aunt Judy: I believe in what I do. I think it matters. My heart is in this work. It's right for me to have been a teacher. I teach in the right ways to get the right results. I used the word *right* a lot, but that's the truth. For me, teaching is about doing what life said is right. It's really a matter of being honest with myself and of listening to my heart and soul. My conscience has been my guide as I sought to do what's right. I think I have the conscience of a teacher.

Katy: You sure have taught me a lot today and all of my life. Thanks a lot, Aunt Judy.

Aunt Judy: My dear Katy, you are so welcome. It's a joy to teach you. Now before you go I need you to teach me something. This computer is acting strange. Your generation knows all about these things. Show me what I am doing wrong, please.

Katy: I would be glad to. Imagine it. I get to be your teacher. This is so cool.

Why was it mandatory for Judy to be a teacher? How did she realize and confirm that teaching was mandatory for her? What would have happened had she not returned to teaching? What happened because she did return to teaching?

What can Katy do to further identify whether teaching is the best career choice for her and whether she is a person who schools need as a teacher? How can Katy know with absolute certainty that she should select teaching and that teaching should select her?

One person looks at the work of a teacher and says, "I could never do that." The statement is sincere, honest, and accurate. When a person evaluates any career and concludes, "I could never do that," it is a revealing decision that should be obeyed. It is mandatory for some people not to teach.

Another person considers teaching and notices some positive aspects of being a teacher yet notices with much concern some negative aspects of being a teacher. "I'm really good at math. I used to be a math tutor when I was in middle school. I took all the tough math classes in high school. Math is my major in college. But lots of companies hire math experts, and they pay so much more than schools pay. Plus, you can get promoted, and you can buy stock in the company. I'd probably be a good teacher, but I don't know about working at a school. What do you do with the students who cause trouble? I think I would be better off at a company working with adults." That is very realistic. Teachers work with children and teenagers, and for some people that applies their skills while for others that is the wrong work environment.

Yet another person views teaching with eagerness. "I just love children. I've been a babysitter, a camp counselor, a Sunday school teacher, and an elementary school volunteer mentor. Children and I get along so well. Teaching sounds perfect." It might sound perfect because it seems to be an extension of that person's prior work with children, but actually being a full-time teacher in a school that is a formal workplace where laws, policies, regulations, and requirements govern is different from the babysitting or camp counselor experiences. This person has had good experiences in roles that seem to be previews of teaching but that are not identical to teaching. Proceed with eagerness and with many questions to accurately realize what teaching truly demands of you.

What can aspiring teachers do to gain the best possible awareness of what teaching would be like and to confirm or reject the interest they have in teaching? Simulations are useful but not sufficient. Babysitting, being a camp counselor, helping with a Sunday School class, volunteering at a church summer vacation Bible school program, showing a younger brother or sister how to play soccer or how to solve a math problem are good experiences, but they do not equal all aspects of being a classroom teacher.

During the college years it may be possible to substitute teach occasionally. The college schedule and the local schools' schedule may have some days when substitute teaching could be done. This will not reveal everything about being a teacher, but it is at a school and it is with students. Also, it gives you the opportunity to talk with current teachers whose career experiences, insights, and attitudes can provide beneficial understanding. Their experiences do not dictate what your experiences would be, but their thoughts do give you much to reflect upon.

No matter how much the aspiring teacher prepares to be a teacher, the preparation is inadequate. Anticipate a bolt of reality when you move from being a college student taking education classes to a college student in a semester of student teaching to being the teacher.

The first year of teaching will have difficulties. You will consider quitting during the year or when the year ends. For some people that thought is true and should be obeyed. For other people that thought is the evil side of life seeking to steal your vocation. During that first year, get much guidance from colleagues. Every problem you encounter in your first year of teaching or in any other year has been encountered by and solved by another teacher.

When your conscience, your advisors, and life itself convince you that it is mandatory for you to be a teacher, obedience to that mandate can be fulfilling yet punctuated with adversity, hardship, and dismay. Only the strong will thrive.

Being a teacher does not obligate you to be a hero. Do not measure yourself according to whether or not you made the impossible happen. If that is your standard, you will have zero victories and zero accomplishments.

Use a standard that requires you to achieve everything that is possible. Then, when the possible has been reached, determine what new possibilities are attainable given the firm foundation of unprecedented results that you and your students have created together.

The mandatory teaching imperative that the conscience of a teacher hears, knows, and obeys is a calling to accept a profoundly important duty. This mandate does have some idealism in it, or how would the occasional despair or disappointments be endured? However, the mandate puts you in a work setting where reality shouts as idealism whispers. The whispers are gentle reminders of why you are a teacher. The shouts are reminders that this work is very complex work.

Teaching will never be easy. Teaching will always be important. If it is mandatory for you to be a teacher, you will find ways to prevail over the difficulties in teaching because your conscience has led you to the commitment you have to the importance of teaching.

Chapter Sixteen

Seek Wise Counsel

CASE STUDY 1

"The students are so rude. The comments they make to each other are cruel and vicious. They cheat and I give them the zero grade they deserve, and they complain to the principal. He tells me to let them take the test over. That's no punishment. It just shows the students that they got away with cheating. Why did the principal listen to the students and ignore what I had to say? There's so much more that is going wrong. At this rate, my first year of teaching will be my last year of teaching. Can you give me any advice? You've taught for a long time. What can I do to make this better, or will it just always be this bad?" Anne Hart was very frustrated.

Rachel Bell, a teacher with twenty-two years of experience, listened closely and remembered how very difficult her own first year of teaching had been. She also knew that her second and third years were better, or, to be honest, were not as bad but were still strenuous and problematic. She had promised herself to quit at the end of her third year, but the school got a new principal who actually was an instructional leader and who was serious about discipline, so she stayed one more year, and that year went well.

That excellent principal stayed for eleven years and helped make the school one of the best in the state. The next principal was inept, lazy, and a friend of people in power, so he did terrible work and got away with it. This experienced teacher had seen enough ups and downs at her school to know that what her colleague described as the experience of the first year of teaching was true. What advice should she give?

"I cannot promise you that next year will be a big improvement, but you will have some advantages next year that you could not have this year. The fact that you will have taught for one year means you've been through the cycles of a school year. You'll know what to expect. There won't be so many surprises."

"You'll have a year of already finding out what worked and what did not work. You know what your best lessons or tests or homework assignments this year were. You also know what activities you did in the classroom that just did not work. The lessons learned from this year will help smooth out some things next year."

All of that perspective was sincere, but it did not ease the anguish and frustration that plagued Anne. "Rachel, I'm sure those things are true. I have learned a lot this year, but there has been such a price to pay for that learning. I work all weekend, every weekend, and nobody cares. I made a lot of changes in the second semester based on what worked or didn't work in the first semester. I write discipline referrals day after day, and the report I get back usually says the assistant principal had a conference with the student. A conference? The student defies my instruction, uses vulgar language in class, leaves class without permission, and slams the door. The student gets a conference. That undermines my authority. There's only so much I can do, and I'm doing everything I can. This place seems to be so out of control. It's dysfunctional."

"Anne, I understand what you are saying. I've been here twenty-two years. It was awful at first. Then we got a great principal and we really were a school, a serious school. This place is mismanaged, and there is no leadership. The people in charge are good friends, and they take good care of each other so they can keep their high-paying jobs. But their incompetence does not have to completely destroy everything."

"Here's an idea. I meet once each week with a group of about eight or nine teachers. We started this a few years ago. We just trade ideas. We concentrate on what we can control. We tell each other about the lessons we used recently that worked great so everyone gets good ideas. We tell each other about our lessons that weren't so good, and we figure out how to do better. We advise each other on discipline actions to take in the classroom. It's a real help to find out what other people do that works. Please join us tomorrow right after school in my room. I'm sorry we did not get you involved sooner, but during the last two months of this school year I hope this group can be helpful to you. You'll hear good ideas and some blunt thoughts, but you'll get great advice. We're honest with each other. We encourage each other."

Anne was willing to try anything. "I'll be there. Even if I quit after this year, I want April and May to be less brutal on me and more productive for the students. By the way, do the school administrators know about your group?"

Rachel grinned in a way that said as much as her words expressed. "Yes, indeed. We told the principal and the assistant principal plus the school counselors about the group when we started meeting. We invite them to join us. They never do. The principal has told me he just can't fit our meeting into his schedule, but he has the time. He sits in his office a lot during the day, and after school he often visits practices of the athletic teams. He used to be a coach."

"I do know that the principal tells the school district officials about our group. He tells them how this school has such a wonderful faculty that solves problems together because he has empowered us and trusted us to be leaders. Of course, he's just telling them what they want to hear and what he wants them to hear. It's a shame that things like that happen. We can't change that. Our group concentrates on what we can control. It's been helpful to me. Please join us. You'll get good ideas. Plus you'll find out that it's not just first-year teachers who have battles and frustrations."

Anne had one more question. "Rachel, I'll be there. I'll do anything. Things just can't continue like this. One other thing. Does your group have a name?"

Rachel smiled with confidence and joy. "Yes. The name came from one of our discussions at a meeting during our first year of doing this. We call ourselves SAVE. Our goal is to learn continuously. We never make announcements about our meetings, but we welcome everyone. We are informal, but we are serious. I really wish you had known about his earlier, but now that you know I think this will be helpful. All the teachers in SAVE learn from each other. You will learn, and other people will learn from you. One rule is that we never mention names. Another rule is that we never gripe. We know that some people here don't work much or get much done. We know there is a lot to complain about. We do not spend time on that. Comments about other people would be unprofessional. Complaining about what we can't change is a waste of time. We concentrate on what we can control. We want to know what works best in classrooms. Our concentration is on teaching students. I'm so glad you will be there tomorrow, Anne."

"Thanks, Rachel. You've given me some hope. By the way, does SAVE stand for something? It's a neat name. What's it mean?"

"Sincere Advice Is Vital for Educators. We give each other advice, ideas, encouragement, help. We're in a difficult career, but we are determined to save ourselves from unnecessary problems and failures and frustrations. We united to save students from mistakes they don't have to make or from achieving so much less than they could. That's who we are and what we do. We really do save each other a lot of anxiety and headaches."

Anne was hopeful. "That's just what I need. Someone to save me. Thanks so much. I can't wait to get all of that sincere advice."

CASE STUDY 2

Anne returned for a second year of teaching. The SAVE meetings she attended in April and May of her first year as a teacher made Anne aware of much that she never had known. Every teacher at the SAVE meetings acknowledged problems. Some of those problems were more serious than others, but there was not one problem-free classroom in the school. Anne was not alone, as she had once suspected, in facing incorrigible students, endless interruptions of class when the front office or the school counselors or some field trip took students out of classes, or when facing a limited—sometimes nonexistent—work ethic from some students.

SAVE meetings were never times merely to share the miseries of everyone or of anyone in attendance. SAVE was dedicated to sharing or creating successes. Every teacher at each SAVE meeting was required to report some good news. Teachers brought copies of lessons or instructional materials that had worked especially well. Teachers told about how a lesson had been modified based on ideas from a SAVE meeting and if the results were favorable.

At one meeting in November of her second year in teaching, Anne was the first person to speak. She was excited as she explained some good news.

"One student I have in eleventh-grade English class failed my class last year. You would think that when the counselors make schedules for students they would notice that and assign the student to a different teacher for when they take the class over again. Apparently no thought is given to that. Why expect the second year of the same situation to work better than the first year did?"

"Well, I noticed this when I came back to school in August. I immediately talked to two school counselors. They said it happened all the time. They even said they were too busy to check the schedule of each student who failed a class to be sure they had a new opportunity with a different teacher. I took their comments to mean that my concern was of no importance."

"I asked an assistant principal if he thought it made any sense for a student to be back in the same classroom with the same teacher for a second time. Wouldn't the student think 'This is a classroom where I failed before? I'll probably fail again?' He had no real answer. Obviously, nobody was going to do anything, so it was up to me. I had to deal with this."

"You'll remember I asked for advice at the first SAVE meeting this year. The advice has made such a difference. You told me to talk with teachers who had taught this student in classes where he passed the class or did better than just passing. I was supposed to find out what worked then. You also told me to talk to teachers whose classes he had failed if, in fact, that had happened. You were right. He failed two classes in ninth grade and two classes in tenth grade. I read his complete student folder. He failed classes in middle school. He struggled in elementary school."

"I decided to find out if there was some reason. Is he lazy? Is he involved with the juvenile justice system? You know what the answer is? He can barely read. He is a seventeen-year-old high school junior, soon to be eighteen years old. His reading test scores always put him at the bottom of the wide range for normal. It's not going to stay that way."

"I talked with our school's reading specialist. For whatever reason this student never received specialized reading instruction in middle school or high school. Those fancy reading tests the students take always showed he was at the lowest level in the normal range so no intervention ever happened. So much for those tests helping him. Well, intervention is happening now."

"The reading specialist and I set up a plan. On Friday of each week I give her all of the work we will do in class for the next week. My student spends my class time on Monday with the reading specialist. She is building his overall reading skills, and she prepares him for our work that we do the rest of the week. She has some other students at the same time she works with my student, but her class is designed for individualized instruction anyway."

"He is not failing eleventh-grade English now. He has turned in every assignment. He has a grade of C, and it is not far from a grade of B. I was very honest with him when the school year began. I told him that I figured he probably hated being back in eleventh-grade English in the same classroom with the same teacher. He sure agreed with that. I got his attention."

"Then something else happened. I told him that another teacher mentioned to me that he was very talented in art. He just has a natural ability. She knew this because he did great work on a project in her class where students could draw a poster about some event in U.S. history or write a paper about the event. The poster had to have four different scenes in it to really show how some event developed. His drawing was fantastic."

"So, he still has to write papers for English class, but I give students the option, for example, to write a two-page paper or to write a one-page paper and include a separate, detailed illustration that expresses artistically the main idea they put into words. Giving them a choice seems to work. The truth is, some of the illustrations are really powerful. Maybe half of the class picks the illustration option. Some articles or books use text and pictures, so this is real world."

"They still have to write, but the students who draw seem to write better now than at the start of the year. They do their drawing first and then they can more successfully put into words what they see that they put into a picture."

"So, there's my good news, the SAVE advice sure did save me from what I thought would be a hopeless situation. Look what that advice enabled the student to experience. Thank you to everyone here. And you may want to use that illustration idea with some of the assignments you give students. We even have some short in-class projects where the students work in groups and what they turn in has to include an illustration they create. The critical thinking they do together is impressive. It's been very encouraging to me."

"It's taught me a lot. I think that when teachers team up and encourage each other and trade ideas, we can do so much more than when we just fight battles alone in our classroom. Teaching is still really difficult work, but doing the work together makes it more possible to survive and sometimes to have a big success."

The group smiled, applauded, and felt inspired. Rachel spoke next. "What Anne just told us is a perfect example of why we started SAVE. We don't get paid to attend these meetings. We give our time voluntarily for these meetings. We do this because it's the right thing to do. It's practical. It's better than any of the professional development programs we have to attend. We are here as professionals, as colleagues, as friends helping each other so we can help our students more. Schools should do more of what we do in SAVE. I hope the example we set will catch on. What we are doing is right; it's just the right thing to do. That's why it works."

The SAVE meeting continued for over an hour. There were more good news reports. There were questions asked. There were ideas shared, traded, and created. Real solutions were found to real problems, but if those solutions were not completely successful then more work would be done at the next SAVE meeting to find an improvement.

Rachel's thought about what the SAVE group does is correct. What they do is right. How they do it is right. The impact of their shared endeavor is right.

For the SAVE group, doing what is right was not mandated by law, policy, regulation, or by a directive from school administrators. These teachers are doing what is right because their students benefit and because they themselves benefit. The conscience of a teacher says to do what is right. The right work done in the right way for the right reasons gets the right results.

Anne, Rachel, and their colleagues each listened to their individual conscience. They have created a true community of learners who have formed a shared standard of conscientiousness. They have individually and collectively confirmed, experienced, and manifested the power of the conscience of a teacher. They have not eliminated or solved all of the problems in their school or in education everywhere, but they are making a difference, they are touching the lives of students and of each other, they are seeking wise counsel, providing wise counsel, and applying wise counsel. They surpass the obligations of their employment contract as they honor the shared commitments of their mutual contract with each other and as they individually listen to their conscience.

Chapter Seventeen

Getting More

We get more of what we reward. The reward need not be money or fame; the reward need not be prizes or publicity. Simply being noticed, being acknowledged, or being appreciated can warm a heart, inspire greatness, or create a powerful moment. The conscientious teacher looks for ways to create such moments.

There are students who always behave properly at school, and they always get their work done. They obey rules, and they follow instructions. They cause no problems. They are a pleasure to know, to teach, and to interact with. Far too often these cooperative, mannerly, accomplished students get no acknowledgment of their proper behavior and their excellent efforts.

These exemplary students should get more than avoiding trouble and punishments. They do not need false praise or ego boosters. They simply deserve polite, sincere, caring expressions of encouragement and appreciation. A note written on their homework paper saying "The questions you asked in class today were outstanding. Keep up the great work!" is a good way to let your student know that his or her effort is noticed.

"Great question. Really good thinking," can be said to a student whose insightful query in class created new learning for everyone. We get more of what we reward. We get more of what we encourage. We get more of what we compliment.

Athletes and athletic teams in schools often get the most vigorous support, cheers, and recognition. Is that how it should be? Is that right? Should a school celebrate touchdowns more than superior grade point averages? Should athletic achievement get banquets, pep rallies, awards, publicity, and support while academic achievement might get a generic certificate?

Will students, teachers, school administrators, parents, and guardians attend athletic events to cheer for their team? Yes, and they should. Will those same people equally cheer for students as students, attend classes to see their son or daughter learn and be as noticeable throughout the instructional part of school as they are at the sports facilities?

That would mean that parents and guardians who attend athletic events at school require themselves to visit classes at school. That would mean teachers who also coach a sport would always put more effort into causing learning in their classes than causing athletic success in their sports.

What is a conscience-driven teacher to do in the midst of a society that reveres sports and that acclaims athletes? Constantly show in everything you do that teaching and learning are the ultimate events at school. Acknowledge minute-to-minute academic achievements. Communicate to students the worthiness of their efforts. Do not mislead students with false praise, but do not overlook opportunities to offer earned recognition.

Conscientious teachers work hard, but rarely are they told that they are appreciated. Some teachers arrive at school early, well before the school administrators do, but it is unusual if those extra hours are valued by anyone except the teacher who is not seeking tribute but who would be quite pleasantly surprised by being told "Thank you for the extra effort you make daily."

That thank you will seldomly be heard, so a conscientious teacher has to thank himself or herself daily for the great work being done. Be honest and compliment yourself only when it is earned, but give yourself the praise you deserve. "That was a great question I asked, and the discussion that followed was brilliant" is an example of an internal thank you.

CASE STUDY 1

It was the part of a faculty meeting when the principal opened the discussion to any ideas on any topic with the one goal of improving academic achievement by students. Everyone knew that there were rules to follow. Comments had to be polite, professional, and helpful. Personal comments were unacceptable.

On this day one eager teacher quickly raised her hand to be the first speaker. "I have a question for everyone. What can we do to make getting good grades the thing our students care the most about at school? They get excited about clubs and sports. They get excited about school concerts and the prom. They get excited about coming here before the school day starts so they can do weightlifting and staying after school for hours to have marching band practice. But there aren't many students who are excited about learning and about doing the real work it takes to honestly earn a good grade."

That question rapidly got some responses. One teacher said, "It would be great to think we could do that, but how likely is it for high school students to have the same enthusiasm for a science project that they have for a touchdown or a home run?"

Another teacher replied, "That's exactly the point. Look at what signals we send to the students. How many of the announcements each day are something about sports or clubs? Those things need their publicity, but it starts to look like sports and clubs are the only important events."

One teacher added this thought: "This school lets students miss class for so much stuff. They go tutor at the middle school. They go to fund-raising events during the school day that we let them buy tickets to and miss class. We interrupt classes all day with announcements over the PA system. We never interrupt club meetings or sports practices. We let students miss class all the time, but we tell them education is important. We really need to be consistent so our actions match our words."

The principal asked the next question. "These are interesting thoughts. Who has an idea of some action to take?'

The teacher who taught a television broadcasting and journalism class spoke next. Her class creates the daily school announcement television show, which is a four-minute broadcast shown throughout the school at the end of each day. "Let's do what companies do to advertise their products. Let's use television. Let me know what is going on in your classrooms, and my journalism class can come do a news story. We could even do commercials about homework assignments or projects or tests."

The teacher who organizes the Homecoming Week events had a suggestion. "We make Homecoming Week a big deal, but we never have a week like that for anything related to academics. Maybe each department could sponsor a day or a week when there are unique ways to promote that department. For Homecoming Week we have a day when students dress in 1950s styles since our school opened in 1954. Maybe the social studies department could sponsor a history dress-up day and students dress like famous people in history or like people did at certain times in history."

The discussion continued. All of the ideas were emailed to the faculty and staff the next day. The school's climate committee and student achievement committee were each given the responsibility of following up on half of the ideas and reporting their thoughts at the next faculty meeting.

Schools get more of what they reward most, celebrate most, publicize most, and recognize most. Conscientious teachers could conduct a school priority audit to measure all of the school's messages to students about what is important. The audit could evaluate how often and why classes are interrupted versus how often instructional time is protected so there are not interruptions. The audit could review the daily announcement program to see what topics get the most attention and what topics get little or no attention.

One possible result of the audit could be a revelation that classes are frequently and unnecessarily interrupted, which results in less instructional time. The audit could show that some students miss several days' worth of classes when events or meetings, field trips, or fund-raisers allowed them to be out of class. The audit could show that the school's actions about its priorities do not exactly match its words, mission statement, or other claims about its priorities.

A conscientious teacher can do a classroom audit to measure and to evaluate how time is used, how stated priorities are or are not consistently implemented, how efficiently time is used versus minutes here and there that evaporate with nothing being accomplished.

Schools can implement various programs, campaigns, and initiatives to get more of the desired results. Some of these may be effective, while others fail. Some schools may never make any effort toward a comprehensive plan to be a fully unified organization that uncompromisingly makes each decision and takes each action to support the purpose of causing learning.

It helps when everyone at a school, every decision at a school, and every action at a school supports the school's purpose; however, that does not often happen. What's a conscience-driven teacher to do amid a school that contradicts itself with actions that limit, hamper, or sabotage instruction and learning?

One answer is to magnificently control what you can control. Make everything done in your classroom completely dedicated to causing learning.

Another answer to consider is that it might be necessary to teach elsewhere. If a school is so dysfunctional that no matter how hard you work, how many hours you invest, or how devoted you are, the organization you are part of undermines your effort, it is unhealthy, unproductive, and unwise to stay there. Sometimes getting more requires getting out.

Chapter Eighteen

Good News

The following emails are good news that conscientious teachers could email to parents or guardians of students:

FIRST EMAIL

"This is Ms. Simpson. I teach the U.S. History class that David takes. I wanted you to know how impressive his work was on the test we had yesterday. There were forty multiple-choice questions and one essay question. He had thirty-nine of the forty multiple-choice questions right. His essay was perfectly thought out and perfectly written. He really understands the facts of history and the ideas of history."

"He analyzes events with a scholarly depth and with precision. He also has great class participation. He is always prepared for class, he always pays attention, and he asks insightful questions. I wanted to keep you informed about the outstanding work he is doing. One other thing—his behavior is exemplary. He is polite, and he follows all rules or instructions."

SECOND EMAIL

"Hello. This is Mr. Spencer. I teach the seventh-grade math class that Caroline is taking. It has been about a month since I was in touch with you, so I wanted to provide an update. She is making great progress in math. The first semester was a struggle for her, then in November when she started coming each Tuesday and Thursday for the extra math session before our first period class, everything has become much better for her."

86 Chapter 18

"Some of the algebra equations we worked on recently were not at all simple, but Caroline actually helped explain them to everyone in the class. She understood the concepts perfectly. She has told me how interested she is in basketball, so she has been analyzing basketball statistics from the teams at our school. I think that the coaches would like to hire her. Her analysis of their statistics has helped the teams and individual players realize what they need to work on. Her grade in the first semester for math was 79 percent, which is a C, but in this semester so far she has a 94 percent, which certainly is an A grade. I wanted to share this really good news with you."

THIRD EMAIL

"Hi. This Ms. Fontaine. I would like to be sure that all of the parents and guardians of my fifth-graders know of our next big project. Each student has selected a career that interests them. They are doing research on that career. They will learn the history of this type of work, the educational requirements for this type of work, and the license or certification or other credentials that are required to do this type of work."

"Also, as part of this project, they are to interview someone who is currently doing the type of work they are interested in. I hope you can help them find someone to interview. Perhaps you can help them arrange to talk with a friend or a neighbor, perhaps a family member, or it could be someone else you know. The interview, of course, is their responsibility, but they may need your help to make arrangements. They will organize all of the information they get onto a big poster like the ones used for science projects and make a presentation in class, or they can organize everything on the computer and show that to us in class. I hope that everyone will learn a lot about careers. Let me know if you have any questions."

The following comments are good news plus some encouragement and guidance that conscientious teachers could write on papers they grade and return to students.

FIRST COMMENT

"This essay is outstanding. You organized it just like we practiced in class. The sentences and paragraphs are well developed. Your spelling is 100 percent correct and shows how much you have worked on that. The ideas you explained are very interesting. Great work."

SECOND COMMENT

"This is the best test grade you have had this semester! That is fantastic. Those questions you asked in class the day before this test really helped prepare you well. Keep doing a lot of class participation like that."

THIRD COMMENT

"This paper has to be three full pages long, but your paper is only one page. You got off to a great start, but it needed to be finished. You know our rule. Tomorrow you can turn in more work to get partial credit. You need to turn in four more pages, which is double the amount you did not do. You can do that. You'll learn more, and it will help your grade. Tell me if you have any questions."

FOURTH COMMENT

"This paper gets a big, bright, shiny star on it for the wonderful work you did. This spelling test has a perfect score of twenty out of twenty. Way to go."

FIFTH COMMENT

"First, I came to your chorus concert last night. You and all of the singers were as good as professional performers. Second, this poster you created for our World War II project is just as eye-catching as the posters that were used back then. You have very high-quality artistic and creative skills."

SIXTH COMMENT

"You obviously put a lot of effort into studying for this test. You worked really hard in class during our unit on the solar system. That hard work means you got an A on this test. I hope you will always keep working just like that."

Please notice, none of these emails or comments on papers are usually required according to an employment contract. Why do some teachers take the time and make the effort to communicate so effectively with families and with students? One reason is because that is what they hope the teachers of their children do, so they treat their students the way they would like their own children to be treated.

Another reason is because these emails and comments help promote the type of work by students that causes learning. Another reason is because it is good to do. One more reason is because it is right. The conscience of a teacher says to do what is good, do what is right, do what you hope people will do for your children. For a conscientious teacher, there is no alternative.

Begin with the premise that most students at most schools do what they are supposed to do most of the time. Of course, some students are defiant, disruptive, disorderly, and refuse to do any work, refuse to follow rules, or rarely obey instructions.

Those difficult students absorb much time and energy from teachers and school administrators. Those difficult students must be dealt with, and some proper actions must be found to educate them and to correct their behavior. Some of them may need an alternative school to address their needs.

From the many students who do their work, who obey the rules, who follow instructions, much good news is created each day. Notice the good news. Do not let the trouble caused by the few prevent frequent attention for the many who cooperate and achieve.

The conscience of a teacher is aware that good and bad exist in schools. Good and bad decisions. Good and bad behaviors. Good and bad leadership. Good and bad teaching. The conscientious teacher permits himself or herself to do only that which is good, to encourage that which is good, and to address that which is bad. There is good news. Find it and acknowledge it. Cause the learning that creates good results and good news.

Chapter Nineteen

Self-Preservation

Exhaustion is an enemy of greatness. Avoid exhaustion. Fatigue is an obstacle to being productive and effective. Avoid fatigue. Burnout is the mortal foe of achievement. Prevent burnout.

Illness occurs to all people. The best of teachers can get the worst of colds any teacher could experience, the flu, pneumonia, injuries, accidents, or more severe bouts of disease. All of these unfortunate maladies interfere with teaching. Reality is that everyone gets sick, anyone can have an accident, and disease can attack an otherwise healthy person.

In a classroom where several students are sneezing, others are coughing, and another is blowing his nose, it is impossible to protect yourself from contact with the germs that are being spread. Some illness can be managed without missing school, while others require a sick day or sick days. An ill teacher cannot do his or her best work and could spread the illness to others.

Beyond the physical illnesses or conditions that teachers encounter are the mental burdens that the weight of teaching tasks can provoke or incite. The needs of and the difficulties faced by an increasing portion of students grow in frequency and in complexity. A conscience-driven teacher would like to solve all of those real problems impacting real people. No one teacher can do everything that is needed by every student. It is sometimes difficult to be at peace even when you do all you can with what you have where you are.

What can be done to promote the self-preservation of teachers? Assume that employers of school teachers cannot or will not do anything that reduces the demands on teachers. In truth, assume that the demands on teachers will continually increase as the trend of recent decades expands. Given those assumptions as reality, a teacher must manage his or her self-preservation. How?

Starting with the basics can be a good beginning. A well-developed conscience functioning in a healthy body will be enhanced, so how is that physical health supported? There are no secrets to good health. Some of the basics include proper nutrition, regular exercise, and enough sleep.

Can teaching interfere with consistent implementation of those basics? Yes, so teachers have to manage their health or the severe demands of teaching will mismanage your health for you.

Lunch at school is often or always hurried. Lunchtime may be the only opportunity during the school day when a teacher can make an important personal phone call or get caught up on emails. Beware of multitasking during lunch. Lunch can be the only time, in an otherwise unyielding daily series of nonstop responsibilities, when a teacher can pause.

Make lunch a time to be still, eat at a healthy pace, sit down, and visit with colleagues. If the personal phone call is urgent, perhaps it can be efficient and short. If it is not urgent, let it wait until after school.

By lunchtime, a conscientious teacher has worked three or four hours without a pause in the energy-absorbing work of leading groups of twenty-five, thirty, or more children or teenagers to knowledge. The physical demands of teaching can be underestimated. One advantage a teacher can give himself or herself is a duty-free lunch sitting down at a table—not a computer—to eat nutritious food. This is not a time for a soft drink and chips.

At the end of a school day a teacher may have been standing for almost all of eight hours. Standing up for a long time is a requirement in many jobs. Standing up, constantly moving throughout a classroom, managing the behavior of thirty children or teenagers, implementing educational activities for those students, can deplete the energy reserves of anyone.

When the school day ends, a conscientious teacher's work continues. There are papers to grade, meetings to attend, parents and guardians of students to call or to email, lessons to plan, copies to make, and grades to enter in the computer. The teacher who has those duties after school may also have family responsibilities, a doctor's appointment, or errands to run. The teacher may have after-school obligations with a club he sponsors or with a team she coaches at school.

It can easily appear that there is more work to do than there is time in the day to squeeze in everything. Time management is a learned skill. Managing time well can help busy people manage their health.

And then there is sleep or, too often, the lack of sleep. Doing high-quality teaching under the influence of weariness, tiredness, or exhaustion simply does not happen or cannot be sustained. The body needs the healing and restorative process of ample sleep nightly.

There must be a sleep curve that has a point on it where sufficient sleep is obtained and where the necessary work gets done. Too much sleep and some important work is not completed. Too little sleep and the quality of work declines. Find the point on the sleep curve where you get the right amount of sleep that supports the right amount of work.

Students of world history have been taught that some ancient civilizations, such as the Greeks, prized the ideal life as including a healthy mind in a healthy body. Teaching can and does exercise the mind in vibrant, wholesome ways; however, some situations that teachers encounter can tax the mind to or beyond healthy limits. Go one step beyond the Greek ideal to seek a healthy conscience guiding a healthy mind working through a healthy body.

A student you invested much extra time and effort into drops out of school. Two students in your classroom get into a belligerent, vulgar, vicious shouting match. A desk in your classroom is empty because a student is recovering from serious injuries due to a car accident. A desk in your classroom is empty because a student died from a wicked, evil disease. A student's parent sends a totally inaccurate, harmful, and cruel email to you blaming you for everything imperfect in her child, and she copies the principal, the assistant principal, and the school district superintendent. A person speaks at a community forum and slanders you with false accusations that are completely unfounded but that cause irreparable damage to your reputation.

Events such as those can strain or injure the psychological fitness and mental well-being of anyone. Hope that such events never occur, but know that they can, so be prepared.

There will be decisions made by school administrators that are unfair to you, that disappoint you, that discourage you, that make no sense to you, and that are wrong. You may be able to offer your ideas, express your concerns, and get a decision changed, but reality says do not expect significant change in many decisions.

A teacher cannot control the decisions of school administrators. No worker anywhere can control the decisions of managers, directors, supervisors, or executives. Those people may see the organization from a different perspective, and their broad responsibilities may lead to decisions that have to factor in trade-offs.

A teacher can control how much those decisions will be allowed to cause a defeatist attitude. "This school is so mismanaged and misled. This place is just dysfunctional. It's awful." Those conclusions could be accurate, or they could be exaggerated. Mismanagement and misleadership can negatively impact the entire school, but they need not always dominate what a conscience-driven teacher does in her classroom or how a conscience-driven teacher does his classroom work. Maximize any instructional control you still have.

Unless and until the education bureaucracy and the political processes that regulate schools force every teacher to use a prepackaged script daily so that every classroom follows a regimented, uniform, assembly line formula, a teacher can still be the major factor in the classroom.

Conscientious teachers comply with all requirements of law, policy and regulation, but they are not defined by those directives. They define themselves. They shape the experiences in their classroom. They interact with students in the wonderfully human, magnificently wholesome, and forever impactful ways that are right, honorable, good, true, pure, and virtuous.

These teachers hold the vital determinant of their mental health. They have a built-in goodness detector that guides them always to do that which is good, to think that which is good, to exemplify that which is good, to personally manifest the good work that their conscience compels them to do. These teachers, in thought and in action, are true to the ethical standards that superior teachers have always obeyed and that the most respected people in any endeavor have always obeyed.

Listening to and obeying the conscience are essential parts of self-preservation for a teacher. These actions are beneficial for physical health and for mental well-being.

Teaching requires a solid foundation of a very healthy and a very well-cared-for heart, mind, body, and soul. To succeed in self-preservation, take good care of your heart, mind, body, and soul. That will not be done for you. That can be done by you.

Chapter Twenty

The Dictatorship of Data

Is it possible for a person to have a perfectly normal body temperature but not feel well? Could that person also have a normal pulse and a normal blood pressure but continue to feel ill? Why aren't those normal measurements matching with the way the person feels? Additional numbers may help, but some qualitative judgment will be necessary also. Thoroughly talking with the patient could disclose as much or more than data will.

A young couple has been dating for one year. The lady and the gentleman are increasingly fond of one another. In the first six months of dating they had 1.3 dates per week. In the second six months of dating they had 1.8 dates per week. Their phone calls have increased from 3.7 per week to 7.8 per week over the same successive six-month periods. Their text messages have quadrupled over the two time periods. According to this data, (1) are they in love? and (2) should they get married?

Even with much more statistical analysis about the young couple, few if any questions about their feelings for each other or their potential as a married couple can be answered with numbers. "I think I 62 percent love him and he 67 percent loves me" is an unreasonable statement. The presence or absence of love will not be known through data. There are limits to what can be understood with numbers.

Are numbers helpful when seeking to comprehend, to grasp, to know? Yes, of course. Are numbers the exclusive source of truth when seeking to comprehend, to grasp, to know? No.

Beware of the dictatorship of data. Guard against, defend against the stampede of statistics. Note the narrowness of numbers.

Concentrate on people, and the numbers will follow. Concentrating on numbers can paint such a narrow picture of reality that the decisions and actions that follow are not helpful to people or could be harmful to people.

94   Chapter 20

Perhaps because of the barrage of education reform efforts during recent decades and the excessive testing that accompanies those reforms, there is more data about schools than has ever existed. Has that data led to certainty about what schools do well and to precision in identifying what schools need to do better plus how schools need to change so better results occur?

What numbers get the most attention? Are schools measured by the statistics generated from several days of state-government-mandated tests given in April or May? Are schools measured by the grades students earn in classes? Are schools gauged by student attendance rates, student drop-out rates, student discipline statistics? Do those numbers tell the whole story?

What is the dictatorship of data? It is the autocratic control over decisions and actions given to numbers and to the conclusions based on numbers. Should numbers be ignored? No. Should numbers be tyrants? No. What, then, does a conscience-driven teacher do with numbers?

Give numbers their due, but control the impact of numbers because data is not all-knowing and statistics are not omniscient. Quantitative analysis should not be given omnipotent authority over education. Education is about people, not about numbers. Education is of, by, and for people. A conscientious teacher puts people first and uses many resources, numbers included, to serve people.

A teacher has five ninth-grade social studies classes. The areas of emphasis in the class are U.S. government, state government, local government, economics, personal finance, and money management. The semester grades in the five classes after the first semester are shown below:

What insights, conclusions, or questions can be found within that chart? Why did the first period have as many D and F grades as it has A, B, and C grades? What explains the superior grades in the third period class including no D or F grades? Why is the grade distribution in first and fifth period classes somewhat similar to a bell-shaped curve, but in the other classes the grades vastly surpass the bell-shaped curve's normal distribution pattern?

Table 20.1.

	A	B	C	D	F
1st period class	4	6	4	8	6
2nd period class	5	7	5	7	1
3rd period class	7	14	5	0	0
4th period class	6	12	7	1	1
5th period class	4	8	8	4	3
Total	26	47	29	20	11

The totals show that more students made an A or B grade than made C, D, or F grades—what does that mean?

Other questions are raised by the chart but cannot be answered using only the numbers in the chart. Were the grades consistent throughout the semester, or did some students improve while others declined? What did the A and B students do to earn their grades that the C, D, and F students did not do? Did any C grades show improvement by a student who made D and F grades in eighth grade? Was a B or C grade a decline by a student who made straight A grades in middle school but who is struggling with the transition to high school?

Are the overall results acceptable? Are the individual results acceptable? Do changes need to be made by the teacher in the second semester? If yes, what changes? What was done in the first semester that should not change? Do the five classes each need to be taught differently? What impact did student behavior and student work ethic have on the grades? How did these students do in their other classes, and what ideas could teachers of those classes provide?

A chart with thirty numbers on it leads to the above questions and more. Additional data could provide details but will not answer all questions. Some answers will come from the nonstatistical awareness of the teacher who alone knows what each student did or did not do moment to moment, day to day in class.

CASE STUDY 1

"Tasha's social studies grade concerns me. She made a D, but earlier in the semester she had a B, actually very close to an A. Then she skipped school two or three days. She did not turn in several assignments. I spoke with her parents every few weeks, and they checked her grades online often. We have one month left in this semester. What do you suggest?" Ms. Reynolds spoke with much concern about her student in hopes that the school counselor could help answer the question.

Mr. Jefferson shared the concern. "I recently heard from her geometry teacher about the same type of problems in that class. Let's check all her grades so far in this semester. The screen shows us her first progress report after one month and the next two monthly progress reports. Her grades have declined in most classes. She is doing best in English. No decline there; she has a B on each progress report in English. The other grades started as A or B and now are C, D, or F. Something happened. Something went wrong. We see that with more ninth-graders than any other grade. The move to high school can be tough. Even if you start well you can get distracted if you get in with the wrong crowd or some bad influences."

"I'll set up a meeting with her parents and with all of her teachers." Mr. Jefferson would provide helpful leadership, monitoring, and follow-up.

Ms. Reynolds had one more request. "Let's meet immediately, please. Tomorrow or the next day. We need to get this turned around quickly."

That meeting will include a summary of Tasha's grades thus far in her first semester of high school. Any discipline incidents will be discussed, including those resolved by teachers and those involving a school administrator. Her school attendance record will be evaluated. The facts from standardized tests given to all ninth-graders in September and October will be considered. Reports from her middle school records will be available at the meeting. All of this information will form a partial awareness of Tasha's status as a ninth-grade student. Beyond all of these numbers, these statistics, this data, what is needed?

Understanding. Clarity. Meaning. Insight. Some of that knowledge can come from a detailed analysis of what the numbers mean. More of that knowledge will come from the discernment, sagacity, and wisdom of the participants in the meeting. Teachers, the school counselor, family, and for part if not all of the meeting, Tasha herself will interact, think, reason, and conclude.

The meeting will be filled with people more than it will be filled with data. The meeting will not be controlled by the dictatorship of data. The meeting will be guided by the inspiration of insight, the wonder of wisdom, the courageous commitment of concern and the totality of truth that comes from the collective conscience of sincerely devoted people whose shared commitment is to do everything possible to make Tasha the best student she can be.

Data can be helpful to people, but people are the most helpful resource available to people. Oppose the dictatorship of data. Embrace the power within people who are conscience driven. Use data as one of many resources to help serve people, teach students, and improve schools. Remember at all times that the purpose of a school is to cause learning by students, not to cause more analysis of numbers that leads to further analysis of more numbers.

School is about people. Conscientious people create a school culture and a school climate founded upon conscience-driven principles, standards, character, integrity, virtue, and work ethic. What data can do is limited. What conscience-driven people can do is unlimited.

Chapter Twenty-One

Teacher or Administrator?

The work of a teacher is done in a classroom with students. The goal of a conscientious teacher is to cause learning for, by, and with each student. Many hours of effort beyond the instructional school day must be invested by a teacher to ensure that learning happens. Papers must be graded, lessons must be planned, conferences with parents and guardians must be attended, faculty meetings will take time, professional development training programs will be attended or completed online. The hours required to do the work well far surpass the hours in a classroom with students, but the time and the work with students in the classroom create for teachers the pinnacle, the essence, the heart, and the spirit of teaching.

A conscience-driven teacher does the work of teaching with an unlimited enthusiasm for and dedication to students, to learning, and to teaching. Can such a teacher who becomes interested in a career transition to assistant principal, principal, or other position in school administration completely transfer the same conscience-driven enthusiasm, work ethic, virtue, and integrity to duties that are at a school, but that are not purely in a classroom?

The work of a teacher is in a classroom. The work of a school administrator, if done correctly, is primarily about what happens in classrooms. Can a person who finds meaning, inspiration, achievement, and success in teaching also find meaning, inspiration, achievement, and success in school administration? Can the conscience of a teacher function as the conscience of a school administrator? Should the conscience be the constant while the job description is the variable? Is there a purity of conscience that is not a function of duties that vary, but of truths that do not vary?

Some teachers are very much at peace with a career plan that includes teaching and only teaching until retirement from the education profession. Other teachers, at some point in their career even if this was not a consideration initially, get interested in becoming a school administrator. The motives are throughout a wide range.

Some people go into school administration with a crusading conviction that they will correct all that they perceive to be wrong at a school. Some people do the math and conclude that the only way to substantially increase their pay is to leave teaching and become a school administrator. Other people may have plotted a career path that will lead them to administrative work at a school, then at a school district, then at a larger school district, and then at state government.

Some teachers leave the classroom, and although they were dismal failures as teachers and they truly disliked teaching, they somehow get selected to be an assistant principal. Other teachers leave the classroom where they were magnificently successful, and their new hope is to do throughout an entire school the type of superior work they did within their classroom.

Some people go into school administration because they will have no papers to grade and no lessons to plan. Some teachers worked themselves into an inner-circle network of good-old-boys and good-old-girls who, competent or not, select each other for administrative positions. Some teachers become school administrators because they see no reason to do the same work over and over every year for thirty years; rather, they seek a career ladder that requires leaving the classroom to climb the ranks of school administration.

Can a conscience-driven teacher become a conscience-driven school administrator? Yes, if they are a conscience-driven person. The job descriptions and the minute-to-minute duties of a teacher versus a school principal are utterly different; however, while the work to be done is different, how the work is done can be quite similar.

The teacher who always went the extra mile for her students can become the assistant principal who always goes the extra mile for students, faculty, and staff. The teacher who had a special place in his heart for students who seemed to be isolated from others can reach out to those students as a principal as he did when he was a teacher.

The teacher whose classroom was a dynamic, energetic, creative, productive place can make faculty meetings and professional development sessions equally worthwhile.

What a teacher does is different from what a school administrator does. How a teacher does her work can be similar to how an assistant principal or principal does her work. The conscience that guides a teacher to honorable, noble, ethical, virtuous work can lead that same person when he or she becomes a school administrator to do honorable, noble, ethical, virtuous work. The tasks are unalike, diverse, and distinct. The fundamental and foundational guiding principles can be identical.

Conscience is not defined by job description. Conscience is defined by the inherent rightness of good, honor, honesty, integrity, incorruptibility, morality, purity, and virtue.

Yes, the conscience of a teacher can and must travel intact with a teacher who moves into school administration. What cannot travel with that new administrator is constant classroom, instructional, direct contact with, and interaction with students.

Principals and assistant principals must manage the building itself—are the doors secured, is the plumbing working, is the ventilation system working, is the computer system functioning? Even with specialists in those areas on the school staff, the school administrators must oversee such endeavors.

Is the school budget balanced? Did all substitute teachers arrive on time? Are we ready for the faculty meeting today? Have the parents arrived for the 9:30 a.m. meeting? Is the gym ready for the district basketball tournament tonight? Is everything organized for the concert tomorrow night with the school band, orchestra, and chorus? Am I up to date with all classroom observations? Have all the monthly reports been sent to central office? Am I caught up with email? Are the science classes back from their field trip? Why did the bells start ringing ten minutes before class was supposed to end?

Those to-do list topics for a school administrator have little or no similarity with the daily to-do list of a teacher. When a teacher considers leaving the classroom or does decide to leave the classroom, it is vital to be fully aware of the trade-offs.

What is being given up? What is being gained? What experiences and achievements will never occur again? What new experiences and new achievements will be possible? What prior joys and what prior frustrations will be out of reach? What new joys and new frustrations will fill the days? Will there be many joys, or will time mostly be spent on crisis management and reacting to problems that other people cause?

Two significant factors in becoming a teacher are to honestly listen to and to truly obey your conscience. Those factors also apply to becoming a school administrator.

A word of caution to conscience-driven teachers who become school administrators. As a teacher you planned lessons, and you carried out those plans. There were some interruptions or disruptions, but essentially the work you did each day was according to what you planned.

School administrators are obligated to react to situations as they occur. Sure, a principal should have a list of daily tasks he or she intends to do, but the job of a principal includes dealing with unplanned events, actions, problems, or opportunities. How you react to those circumstances is completely in your control, which means those reactions can be based on your knowledge, your experience, law, policy, regulation, and your conscience. What you do may already be determined by protocol and mandates. The way you interact with people as you carry out those protocols and mandates can reveal your heart, mind, integrity, and conscience.

Chapter Twenty-Two

Keep Learning

Learn, learn more, keep learning. Read, read more, keep reading. Study, study more, keep studying.

During the college years or during college plus graduate school, prospective teachers complete an educational program that qualifies them to work as a teacher. Exact requirements vary by state and may include a probationary or temporary conditional license to teach. Successful completion of the first year as a teacher can change the probationary level to a more enduring level.

There is more to learn about teaching, about students, about schools, and about working in schools than can be taught during a college undergraduate program or during a college undergraduate program combined with a fifth-year master's degree program. As with many careers, some or much of what a skilled teacher knows comes from practical and realistic experiences of being a teacher.

Great or good teachers want to learn more. Average or bad teachers need to learn more. Learning must continue beyond the college experience and beyond the graduate school experience.

Conscientious teachers have an inherent awareness of how effective their instruction is for their students. These teachers know what instructional activities are working well, are barely working, or are not working at all. These teachers eagerly and continuously evaluate their work in search of enhancements, improvements, or fine-tuning.

Other teachers may think that the instructional routine and materials they have used for ten, fifteen, or twenty or more years are ample. Why change what has always been good enough? Change because good enough gets a grade of 50 out of 100. Do not settle for ordinary when better is possible and when best can be pursued.

Part of the adventure of teaching and part of the intrigue with teaching that conscience-driven teachers experience is to feed their own hunger for learning. "Last year was good. I'll just repeat all of the same stuff" is unacceptable. "Last year was good. What can I learn so I can make next year great?" is the attitude of a conscientious teacher.

What actions can be taken by a teacher to cause learning for himself or herself? Consider the following list, but please add more ideas to it.

1. Take a highly recommended graduate school class.
2. Earn an additional certification or endorsement so you learn more and so you expand the work you have credentials to do.
3. Read the best books, old and new, about teaching.
4. Meet with colleagues to trade teaching ideas and to share instructional experiences.
5. Selectively attend high-quality professional development training programs.
6. Very selectively attend conferences sponsored by professional education groups.
7. Have another teacher observe you teach a class, and then later you can observe that teacher's class. Help each other evaluate what worked well and what needs to improve.
8. If confidentiality protocols permit, audio record your class and later listen to the recording. What do you hear as an observer of the class that you had not noticed while you taught the class?
9. If confidentiality protocols permit, video record your class and later watch the video to evaluate what you see and notice what you had not seen, noticed, or realized while you taught the class.
10. Ask colleagues if you could observe their classroom to gain new teaching ideas and to see your students in another setting. Seeing how your students respond to different teaching methods could be useful knowledge. Seeing how your students behave in different settings also could be useful.
11. Serve on a school committee that is working on a topic of concern to you.
12. Serve on a school district committee that needs teacher input and will give you the experience of hearing different perspectives.
13. Talk to some of your former students and find out what they remember from your class. Now that they can look back on your class with some perspective of time, what do they consider the most effective activities or teaching methods used in the class? What do they recall as not being effective? Student input can be applicable, but it has to be filtered through the clarifying process that your experience and maturity provide. If students said your class was no fun but they worked a

lot and learned a lot, accept the praise. The goal is not classroom fun. The goal is to cause learning through impactful instructional work.
14. Develop a meaningful professional growth plan that truly adds to your skills and knowledge. Involve an administrator who can be a mentor, and ask for the resources needed to implement the plan.
15. Think. Reflection is powerful. Ask yourself why you use the teaching methods, instructional activities, and classroom materials that are commonly implemented in your classroom. What results from these processes confirm that they are the ideal? What needs to change if the current processes are deemed to be less than ideal?
16. Some, but certainly not all, educational conferences can be beneficial to attend, but be selective and be efficient. Some conferences emphasize golf outings and social events more than serious learning sessions for educators. Resist the temptation to attend the conference in San Diego in January. Sure, it is a beautiful area, and the January weather there may be much better than the winter weather in much of the country, but that does not justify the time and the money involved with such an unnecessary trip. Your conscience says do not go and, to be honest, you already knew not to go. Read a good book on teaching instead.

Be suspicious of email promotions that proclaim the wonders of some training session that is coming to your town for one day only. The session's email advertisement suggests that answers to pressing questions and solutions to perplexing problems will be provided at this $199 session, which costs only $49 if you register today. Save all of the money and the time. Have a meaningful conversation with a colleague instead.

Keep in touch with the most impressive educators who you meet at your school, at conferences, and training sessions. Trade ideas, share concerns, work together via email, and work together in person with many other educators you meet at your school and at training events. That follow-up means the learning will continue.

When each school day is over and your materials for tomorrow are copied and organized, pause to reflect on the day. Learn as you analyze the day.

When each school year is over, pause at length to fully reflect on the year. Gain new wisdom, deep learning, new knowledge as you contemplate the totality of the school year. Identify what you would like to know more about before the next school year starts. See yourself as both student and teacher. Cause the learning you need to happen. Attend quality training sessions, which means do not attend many training sessions that are about trendy nonsense or superficial nonsolutions. Read great books. Read serious articles. Think, reflect, contemplate, learn, conclude, and then start the work that applies your newly gained wisdom that is now added to your prior wisdom.

One way to forever be a teacher who causes learning is to forever be a teacher who seeks to learn and who does continually learn. There is no limit to learning for a person who will make the effort to learn, learn more, keep learning.

Chapter Twenty-Three

It Is Personal

A conscience-driven teacher knows this truth: not everything that comes into the brain should come out of the mouth. It is important to speak selectively, using a cautious internal editing process. This can be especially important when a situation occurs that could easily escalate if poorly chosen words are spoken. That same situation could be contained and a resolution of the matter could begin with wisely chosen words.

"You are the worst teacher ever. You are so unfair to me. I always get low grades here. You always pick on me." The student was angrily yelling at the teacher.

Those accusations made by a student to a teacher, even though they are 100 percent untrue and unfounded, can sting a teacher. It hurts to be verbally attacked. The student is wrong to speak with such viciousness. How is this problem to be solved?

The student's comments cannot be overlooked and dismissed. Disciplinary action will be needed. The student's family needs to be informed. A school counselor may need to meet with the student to determine what provoked such rude comments. The teacher needs to document the incident thoroughly. Perhaps a meeting of the student, parent(s), teacher, school counselor, school administrator, and other teachers of the student will be needed, especially if the student is having behavior and/or academic problems in more than one class.

Those actions can help address the verbally abusive misconduct of the student and related issues the student may have. What about the teacher? What is done to support the teacher to whom the verbal abuse was directed? It hurts to be verbally abused. What will soothe the emotional wounds suffered by the teacher?

To the teacher's credit, she did not escalate the verbal venom. The teacher calmly responded to the troubled student, "Carrie, you have done a lot of good work in this class. Something must be bothering you today. Let's step in the hall for a moment to discuss this."

The student might respond with more verbal abuse. The teacher repeats, "Something must be bothering you today. Let's step in the hall for a moment to discuss this." The teacher is avoiding a debate or an argument with the student.

The teacher knows that her duty is to be the voice of calm and reason. The teacher is not adding to the difficulty with condemning comments to the student. That would serve no purpose. The teacher knows that if her own child became similarly disruptive she would hope that a teacher and other educators would intervene professionally and with concern to correctly discipline the misbehavior and to provide helpful guidance.

Consider the teacher again. She came to school today well prepared to cause learning. Yesterday's tests were graded and were ready to be returned to the students. The lessons for today were precisely planned. Classes had been orderly and productive until one student's outburst disrupted everything. The teacher did not deserve the verbal abuse or the class disturbance.

When the school day ended, the teacher spoke with the student's school counselor who had met with the student after the assistant principal assigned the student to the in-school suspension room for the rest of the school day after the verbal abuse incident. The counselor had checked with several other teachers, who reported recent behavior problems with this usually polite, friendly, and successful student. Whatever was wrong would be discovered, and the school, to the extent it had authority and resources, would work with the student's family and the student to reverse the recent trend.

The astute counselor did say to the very concerned, very competent, very respected teacher, "I'm so sorry this happened. Carrie knows better. We'll hope she has better days. Now, do something good for yourself today. You know that what Carrie said is untrue and unfair, but incidents like these can hurt our feelings and really discourage us. It's hard to not take it personally, so I hope you will realize that Carrie is mad about something else. She just directed her anger at you."

Being told to not take it personally is thoughtful but is insufficient. Carrie's words cannot be erased or deleted. Those few bitter words do not define Carrie, a thirteen-year-old seventh-grader who is prone to the frustrating extremes that can accompany students in the middle school years. Those few bitter words are 100 percent untrue about Carrie's teacher, but the words were spoken, were heard, were given no credence, but can linger in the memory.

The conscience-driven teacher who was the target of Carrie's verbal abuse entered the teaching profession to make a difference, to cause learning.

Carrie needs to learn about proper behavior, and she will be instructed anew on manners, anger, and related topics.

Carrie's teacher should tell herself that she handled the incident correctly according to the school's discipline system, according to how she would want her child to be treated if her child had acted as Carrie did and according to her conscience. The teacher was professional. The teacher's words were neutral. The teacher's actions were proper.

Nonetheless, the teacher was treated very unfairly. Words can wound. Teaching is very interpersonal work. Effective teachers interact continuously with students. Some of the favorable impact that teachers have is based on the curriculum content they present to students. More of the favorable impact that teachers have is based on what they do to help students learn and how they interact with students in the learning process.

Another factor that can increase the favorable impact that teachers have is when teachers go the extra mile. How is this done? A teacher is asked by a high school senior to write a letter of recommendation to accompany an application for a college scholarship. That is a common request, but the student adds in his request these uncommon words: "I need it today, please. Today is the deadline."

There are options. The teacher could say, "I'm really sorry, but there is no way I can get this done today. It takes a few days to write and rewrite a good letter."

The teacher could say, "I don't see how to get that done. This is already a busy day. Maybe this came up suddenly or maybe you procrastinated, but the best I can do is tomorrow."

The teacher may think to himself, "This really is not the moment to give the student a lesson on time management. He needs the letter. He did good work in my class last year. I'll find a way. If my son needed help like this I would hope somebody could sacrifice for him, and then I would give him the time management lesson later."

Teaching is personal. The teacher did write the letter of recommendation for the student. It was done, in part, because the student needed the help. It was also done, with an equal or greater motive, of providing peace of mind for the teacher.

Years ago the teacher had promised himself that he would never settle for good enough or ordinary. He promised himself that he would do extra work and make extra effort for his students. Today's request by a time-management-deficient high school senior gave the teacher a chance to again keep that long-ago promise the teacher made to himself.

Writing the letter now is a personal gift to the student. Writing the letter now is a personal gift the teacher gave himself. The teacher was able to do what the student needed. The teacher was able to do what his conscience had always required. Teaching is personal via the proper and professional interpersonal interactions teachers have with students, families, and colleagues. Teaching is also personal in the way a teacher treats himself or herself.

CASE STUDY 1

A very skilled, very accomplished teacher of thirteen years decided a few years ago that she would like to become a school administrator. She had completed the graduate school program to earn school administrator certification five years ago. She began applying for assistant principal positions four years ago. Three years ago she also began applying for academic dean positions, curriculum coach positions, and anything else that could expand her responsibilities and give her new ways to contribute to education.

During the past four years she had applied for twenty-one positions. She had been given one interview during those four years. The day after that one interview she received the robotic, mechanical, inhuman, bureaucratic email comment, "We appreciate your interest in our assistant principal position. We have decided to go in a different direction."

She continued to teach magnificently. Her students learned. Her colleagues had much respect for her. Parents and guardians of students praised her. The principal of her school nominated her for an outstanding teacher award, which she won. A state teacher's organization honored her as their teacher of the year.

She spoke with trusted colleagues who worked in school administration. She sought their advice and help. "What am I doing wrong? Did I offend someone? Am I blacklisted?" Most people advised her to persist, saying it should work out someday. She was not convinced that someday would arrive.

How should this highly acclaimed teacher deal with the personal frustration and disappointment that accompany twenty-one rejections? Those rejections may be based in part on objective factors, but she is convinced and the facts show that many people chosen for the positions she applied for are not as qualified as she is.

The hiring selection mistakes of people who select less-qualified candidates pollutes the quality of school leadership and school management. These mistakes also take a career toll and a personal toll on the more qualified candidates who are ignored, overlooked, rejected, or, it may seem to be and it may in fact be, discriminated against.

What would the reader do if faced with the circumstances of the teacher in this case study? How would the reader manage the personal toll that twenty-one rejections impose? What advice would the reader offer the teacher in this case study?

The teacher's conscience demands that she continue to teach to the best of her ability. Her disappointments will not be allowed to let her lower the standards of conscience that guide her work. But now she faces a reluctantly realized and disturbing reality—some decisions in education are made as friends take care of friends, as favors are returned, and the good-old-boy and good-old-girl network promotes their members-only inner circle with no regard to more highly qualified outsiders and with no concern about the harm they cause by selecting the wrong person.

That reality is one reason schools achieve less than they could. That reality is a compelling reason why the conscience of a teacher must never tolerate personal compromise of ethics and integrity. That reality is also a reason why the conscience of a teacher must always be wise about the petty, political, mischievous, unethical, unprofessional, dissembling decisions and antieducation actions that do occur but which must not prevail.

For every year the teacher in Case Study 1 teaches, her conscience will prevail in her classroom. If she becomes a school administrator, her conscience will prevail in how she does that work. She has made a personal commitment to conscience. She will prevail as she implements the highest personal and professional standards in her work as a teacher, as an administrator should that day arrive, and always as a person. For her, obedience to conscience is very personal.

Chapter Twenty-Four

Credit or Discredit?

When a high school student takes the ACT or the SAT in anticipation of applying to college, there are no extra credit points that can be obtained on those test scores. When high school students take advanced placement tests, there are no extra credit points that can be added to the scores on those tests.

When middle school or elementary school students take tests to measure their reading or math achievement levels, no extra credit points can be earned. When elementary school or middle school students take placement tests to qualify for exclusive programs, no extra credit questions are included with those tests. On all of the tests mentioned above, the score a student gets is the score the student earned.

When a school has elections for class officers, the winner is based on the election results. A student who lost an election for tenth-grade president by a vote count of 214–206 cannot obtain nine extra credit votes to turn the eight-vote loss into a victory by one vote.

When a middle school basketball team loses a game by one point, there are no ways to get two extra credit points to turn the one-point loss into a one-point win.

A high school's speech and debate teams participate in many competitions. After all competitors have completed their presentation, decisions will be made about which students performed best. Extra credit points are not available.

A middle school's chess team enters a tournament. The intellectual effort, the concentration, and the thinking at work by the students fill the room with mental energy that can be felt. There are no extra credit points available. There are no extra-credit chess pieces for a student who encounters checkmate.

An elementary school instrumental music teacher arranged for her fourth- and fifth-grade musicians to enter a regional elementary school music contest. The practices were serious. The performances at the contest were impressive by all school groups. The judges evaluated each performance and awarded no extra credit points.

With one day remaining in a semester, a student's grade is two points away from an A. She takes the final exam, and with that last grade entered in the computer, her average is still two points away from an A. She asks the teacher what she can do for extra credit to improve her grade. The student earned a grade of B. On what valid basis would the student be given a chance to suddenly increase the grade? Would the student move into the A level of learning by doing a quick quasi-task that was done only to raise a grade, not to raise knowledge?

Extra credit is deceptive. A student whose goal is to make an A knows when each assignment is due, knows when each test or quiz will be taken, knows when class begins and it is time to pay attention and to participate in the discussion, and knows what reading must be done by which date to prepare for class. If all of those responsibilities are carried out at the A level, the student will learn an A. (Related thoughts on building responsibility are in chapter 5.)

An earned A is valid and confirms the importance of good work done consistently. An extra-credited A is suspect and compromises the importance of good work done consistently.

How would a conscientious teacher view extra credit? How would a conscientious teacher who seeks to develop conscientious students view extra credit?

CASE STUDY 1

Math Teacher: I have 148 students. For the first semester, forty-two of them had an A. I was really pleased. It would have been only twenty-six A grades, but the extra credit I let them do brought up sixteen students to an A. Ten of those students would have had a B and six would have had a C. They finally woke up and did something better.

Science Teacher: I never give extra credit to my students. I tell them that scientists don't get extra credit in their laboratories or other work. When scientists conduct an experiment, the results are straightforward. If you hoped results would turn out one way for whatever reason but the results are different, those are the facts. They can't ethically add extra-credit points to change their research results.

Math Teacher: I understand that. It's just that we get evaluated on stuff like this. I had thirty-one students with F grades one week before the semester ended. I gave them tons of extra credit work to do. Most of them had done nothing all semester. The extra credit work got twenty-one of them up to a D, so they passed the class. Nobody will criticize me for having ten students out of 148 fail, but thirty-one failures would have raised questions.

Science Teacher: I just make sure I document everything. I notify the parents or guardians of each student once a month if their student has a grade of C, D, or F at that point. I also send good news emails to let families know of excellent work being done. I give all of my students a monthly printout showing all of the details of their grade. It shows every assignment, quiz, and test. They know the facts. They know where they stand.

A few years ago the principal asked me about students who failed science. I showed her everything I did to keep them informed and to update their families. She was satisfied and actually was impressed with how thorough I had been.

Which teacher is providing a better, more useful, more beneficial, more realistic learning experience for the students? What guides the approach of the math teacher? What guides the different approach of the science teacher? What is the right action for a conscientious teacher to take regarding extra credit?

Which option more effectively teaches responsibility in addition to teaching math or science? Which approach more effectively teaches the subject matter of math or science?

Chapter Twenty-Five

Beyond a Job

For the aspiring teacher, if you see teaching merely as "a job," please reconsider whether you should become a teacher. For the experienced teacher, if teaching has declined into being only "a job," take that as a caution that requires action. Know the warning signals of career difficulty such as lethargy, apathy, burnout, frequently calling in sick when you are not ill, and constant frustration with everything and everyone at school.

If your priority is athletics or other extracurricular activities and you are a teacher only so you can coach or so you can sponsor activities, please find another way to coach or to support other extracurricular activities so another person whose top priority is teaching can teach. Another solution would be to make teaching your top priority and then give sports or other activities the lower priority. Both duties can be done well, but teaching is much more important.

There are some aspects of being a teacher that match the features of a job in terms of employment. To become a teacher, a person must complete a job application, must get letters of recommendation, must be interviewed, must be selected among the candidates who were interviewed, must be offered the job, must accept the job, and then complete all paperwork plus training or orientation before reporting for the first day of work.

Interviewing for some jobs can involve negotiating the terms of employment, the terms of a contract, salary, benefits, work schedule, sick days, personal days, vacation days, and the date to begin work.

Employment as a teacher rarely includes any individual negotiation. Private schools may have some variables that can be discussed. Public schools that are governed by laws, regulations, policies, salary schedules, protocols, and precedents do not give the potential employee much or any standing to negotiate. An aspiring teacher is usually delighted with getting a teaching position, even though it is a teaching position that has employment details that may not be ideal.

Experienced teachers also often have little leverage. The salary schedule establishes wages for teaching. The school district calendar shows when the workdays begin and end for each school year along with various professional development days, teacher in-service or records/conference days, and holidays.

"I've been at this school for twelve years. I have always had twenty-four minutes for lunch. I would like to have forty minutes for lunch next year." If a teacher made that request to a principal, the bottom-line response will be "the lunch schedule is set up for the entire school. It cannot be individualized. I realize that twenty-four minutes means a quick lunch, but it's the same for every teacher."

An experienced second-grade teacher may ask to teach third grade next year, and that could be possible. A seventh-grade math teacher who is also certified in science may ask to teach science next year, and that could be done. Nonetheless, many aspects of the employment details of teaching are non-negotiable by any individual.

To be blunt, the terms of employment are take it or leave it. It is important to know these employment realities before considering teaching as a career to determine whether the inflexible terms of employment are acceptable to you or are unacceptable.

There are other aspects of teaching that match typical employment characteristics, including a required time by which to arrive daily, an allowed time to leave daily, other nonteaching duties that are assigned such as hallway supervision or bus duty, being evaluated by school administrators, completion of required paperwork, and attendance at required training sessions.

Despite these job traits of teaching, being a highly effective teacher means seeing teaching and doing teaching as more than a job. The conscientious teacher takes the work of teaching beyond a job description to an imperative of the conscience. The job description tells a teacher what he or she is required to do. The conscience of a teacher leads an educator to the higher level of what can be done. *Can be* surpasses *required*. If *can be* is most effectively implemented, the pursuit of, the commitment to, and the attainment of what can be done far surpasses what is required for a teacher to do.

Conscience-driven teachers expect themselves to achieve all that can be done. They are never personally or professionally satisfied with doing merely what is contractually required. The contract must be honored for legal and professional reasons, but the contract sets the minimal acceptable terms for employment. The conscience must be obeyed for reasons of ethics and integrity. The conscience sets much higher terms.

Abiding by the employment contract is necessary, is proper, is respectable, and is correct. Abiding by the contract with your conscience to do more, to do better, to make a difference, to make a meaningful and good impact, to honorably touch lives is to take teaching far beyond being merely a contract-defined job into being the manifestation of your career's purpose.

At a program to pay tribute to teachers and other employees who are retiring from a school district, a short statement could be read about each person who is retiring. The following statement will not be read about anyone: "He always obeyed his contract."

What will be said? Statements such as "Ms. Anderson always arrived at school early. There were improvements to make in a lesson based on a new idea she had the night before. A student may have a question and needs some tutoring. She has lived a wonderful and meaningful life outside of school as a devoted wife, mother, and grandmother. She is active in her church and in several community groups. At school, she has been a silent superstar, never seeking recognition but always seeking ways to help students. To Ms. Anderson, teaching was much more than a job. Teaching was her life's work, and she has shown all of us how to do this work perfectly."

At a program where students get to honor the best teacher they ever had, the statement read by students will not include, "He showed up on time. Mr. Woodford obeyed his contract. He did his job." The statements will be about a teacher, Mr. Anthony, who "demanded that I do my best work. He never gave up on me. He always encouraged me. He was always there for me. He helped me. He helped me get a scholarship to college. I owe him so much."

Mr. Anthony would not agree that he is owed anything by the student except hard work and cooperation. Mr. Anthony owed himself the personal obedience to being the type of teacher his conscience told him to be. Teaching is not Mr. Anthony's job. Teaching is Mr. Anthony's imprint on lives and on life itself.

Mr. Anthony is not superhuman. He is not heroic. He does not work eighteen hours a day. He does not work 365 days per year.

Mr. Anthony is an exemplary teacher. He does what great teachers have always done. He challenges students. He uses a variety of instructional methods and activities. He is enthusiastic about students, about teaching, about learning. He is available to provide extra help. He makes learning fascinating. He fulfills his employment contract and his conscience contract.

Mr. Anthony lives a meaningful life outside of school. He is devoted to his family. He has several hobbies. He and his family do volunteer work in the community. He is not married to his work; rather, he is conscientiously dedicated to his work.

Mr. Anthony has, listens to, and abides by the conscience of a teacher. Because of that, his teaching work is seen as and is done as much more than a job. For Mr. Anthony, teaching goes beyond a job that is defined by a contract. For him, teaching is a personal purpose that is defined by a conscience.

Chapter Twenty-Six

Keeping Promises

The final evaluation of a teacher is not based on two classroom observations during a teacher's concluding year in a thirty-two-year career of teaching. The true, final, culminating evaluation of a teacher is the cumulative, comprehensive, panoramic set of conclusions that the teacher reaches about his or her overall career achievements.

When a teacher retires to conclude a long career in education, finishes the final day at school, and walks out of the school never to be a full-time teacher again and perhaps never to enter a school again, what are the thoughts that flow through the mind of this person? Is there a sense of peaceful satisfaction of knowing that everything that could have been done for students was done? Is there a sense of fatigue accompanied with relief? Are there regrets about missed opportunities? Is there an overall sense of success or failure?

School districts and/or state governments create processes, procedures, and forms that are used to provide an evaluation system for teachers. These systems can range from the bureaucratic, formulaic, mechanical, rote, and superficial to the purposeful, practical, useful, meaningful, personal, thorough, and real.

Conscience-driven teachers have their own evaluation system that measures the quantity of, the quality of, and the impact of their work daily. The conscience-based evaluation far surpasses the routine evaluation systems used in schools.

The conscience-driven teacher who consistently passes and goes beyond the conscience-based evaluation will have the daily satisfaction that comes from work done well. This teacher will, at the end of a career, have pure peace knowing that decades of honorable teaching work touched the lives of thousands of students.

No matter how many years of experience a teacher has thus far, if the teacher remains in teaching for a full career there will be three decades or so of schoolwork done in that career. Before starting a teaching career, what promises can and should a new teacher make to himself or herself? Consider the list below, and then add to the list.

1. I will never give up on a student.
2. I will challenge my students.
3. I will teach this year's students, today's students with the instructional methods that work best for them.
4. I will arrive early every day.
5. I will be completely prepared with high-quality instructional activities each day.
6. I will grade all papers promptly and thoroughly. I will return all papers to students quickly so the work is still fresh on their minds.
7. I will never use improper, vulgar, or hateful language. I will selectively and precisely control what I say and how I say it.
8. I will teach my students with the same devotion, concern, and commitment that my most outstanding teachers showed when they taught me.
9. I will notice when a student is struggling academically, and I will intervene.
10. I will notice when a student can do much more or can do much better than the student is now doing, and I will intervene.
11. I will become aware of the wholesome interests, talents, and achievements of my students. I will connect those life experiences with what we are learning whenever possible.
12. I will teach by example. My work ethic, my eagerness to learn, and my behavior will form an educational paragon.
13. I will intervene with students who are at risk of failing. I will intervene with students who are never challenged and who are eager to learn but for whom most schoolwork is painfully ordinary or repetitive.
14. I will make students aware of opportunities at school that they are not taking advantage of.
15. I will make phone calls, send emails, write letters, or visit people to help students as they seek summer jobs, as they apply for college, or when they apply for competitive merit-based programs at school.
16. I will follow laws, regulations, policies, and administrative instructions or directives.
17. I will politely and diplomatically, but earnestly and intentionally, express ideas that could improve the management of our school, our school district, and our state's educational system.
18. I will keep in touch with parents and guardians of students.

19. I will grade student work objectively and accurately. I am grading their work, not how likable their personality is or how correct their behavior is.
20. I will work with colleagues. Teachers should not work in confinement and isolation. I will trade ideas with, create ideas with, address concerns about school with colleagues.
21. I will seek wise advice and counsel. The knowledge and the experiences of people at my school are valuable resources that I will benefit from.
22. I will, after I have some experience, reach out to first-year teachers. A first-year teacher has many arduous and taxing realities to master. I will offer ideas, guidance, and encouragement.
23. I will work hard and I will get great results, but I will take good care of myself so my health and well-being are enhanced through this work, not despite of this work.
24. I dedicate myself to causing learning to occur by each student on each day.
25. I will dress, speak, behave, and work professionally.
26. I will do more than is required. I will do better than is required.
27. I will not be discouraged when my extra effort and my good results are unnoticed and unappreciated. I am not doing this work to be noticed or to be appreciated. I am doing this work because I chose teaching and teaching chose me.
28. I will not gossip about students, families, colleagues, or anyone else.
29. I will teach my students as I hope teachers of my own children teach.
30. _____.

The urgency, the difficulty, the problems of the moment can continue to dominate all attention and effort. When that happens, work is reduced to continuous reactions to what occurred instead of purposeful implementation of what is intentionally designed.

Problems do occur despite the best preparation and the most determined work ethic. Work through the problems and return to the intended, purposeful endeavors.

Promises made to yourself do not prevent problems that you did not cause from arising. Promises made to yourself do give you a reason to rise above the problems.

No matter how many years away your retirement from teaching is, take a moment now and identify what you intend to think of your career on the day you retire. Now, what needs to be done at each moment of each day during your career as a teacher to result in the certainty that when you do retire you will have kept the promises you made to yourself about the type of teacher you would be?

By keeping the personal promises to yourself day to day over the course of a career, students benefit as learning is caused. By keeping those promises, you satisfy the conditions placed upon you by your conscience. By keeping those promises, everyone wins, now and always.

Chapter Twenty-Seven

Diligent Excellence

Actions based on conscience are integrated by a unifying theme—doing what is right. The conscience will not direct a person to work effectively one day and to be lazy the next day.

The dictates of and the directions from a conscience guide the thinking of a conscientious teacher. Those thoughts must be followed by actions that implement the thoughts. To maximize results, the ethical urges of a conscience direct the honorable thoughts of a mind that lead to excellent actions that obtain superior results.

For those superior results to be achieved, much work, much labor, much toil, much exertion must be invested. The ethical yearnings of a conscience that lead to the honorable concepts in a mind are merely philosophical wonders until they are enforced by work that puts them into meaningful action.

Teaching well involves doing an abundance of labor. The greatest intentions, the most inspiring idealism, the highest hopes, the loftiest aims, the most noble goals evaporate unless they are translated into actions that are actually carried out.

Consider the following list of tasks that teachers must administer, and then add to the list.

1. Prepare lessons and prepare all of the materials that will be used with the lessons.
2. Type quizzes, tests, projects, assignments, study guides, and daily instructional materials. Make copies of these typed items.
3. Keep the classroom clean and organized.
4. Grade papers. Grade papers promptly and correctly. Record grades accurately in the computer, and, perhaps, in a written grade book. Return papers promptly.

5. Schedule times when your class or classes will go to the library or to the computer lab. Prepare the students for the work to be done there. Prepare all materials the students will need to do that work.
6. Attend meetings before or after school, sometimes with little or no notice.
7. Attend conferences with parents, guardians, school counselors, sometimes with little or no notice.
8. Adjust to interruptions during the school day as students are called over the public address system to leave class, as field trip groups leave or return, as students arrive late or leave early.
9. Create a make-up test for students who were not in class the day of a test.
10. Grade writing work done by students and include detailed comments about the content of the writing, the quality of the writing, and the mechanics of the writing.
11. Supervise in the hallways. Supervise in the bus loading area.
12. Teach classes.
13. Provide work for students who are absent and whose family will pick up missed assignments.
14. Complete surveys sent by state government, by the school district, and/or by the school.
15. Attend professional development and other training programs. View all such programs online as required.
16. Stay current with all new uses of technology.
17. Complete and implement a professional growth plan annually.
18. Create a make-up semester exam for a student whose family will travel during the final exam days.
19. Write letters of recommendation for students who are applying for jobs, scholarships, or college.
20. Attend a meeting of teachers who are in your grade level, on your teaching team, or in your department.
21. Implement a new directive from the school administrators requiring everyone who teaches the subject or grade you teach to use a regularly scheduled test that you and your colleagues write and grade. Report the results of the test to the school administrators so they can evaluate if all students in all classes are progressing without regard to who their teacher is or if some groups are not progressing as well as students who have certain teachers.
22. Provide additional copies of materials to students who lost, forgot, or just did not bring materials to class.
23. Read and study so you expand your knowledge of what you teach and your awareness of various ways to teach that subject.

24. Distribute materials to students as required by the state government, the school district, or the school administration.
25. Supervise a group of students on any day when grade-level or full school testing is done. These tests, required by various levels of government, always consume time otherwise allocated to teaching, so despite the lost hours, be sure students learn every part of the expanding curriculum. Obey all test protocols perfectly.
26. Respond to emails promptly.
27. Update the online posting regularly so students and their families can check on what work is being done in your classroom and what due dates have been scheduled for work that has been assigned.
28. Comply with all requests for information from the school office, the school administrators, or the school district.
29. Make all plans for a substitute teacher, copy all materials for a substitute teacher, and submit a request for a substitute teacher for any day that you will be absent.
30. Complete all required forms, paperwork, and accounting during the first few days of a new school year.
31. Answer the phone, although it disrupts your teaching, when someone in the office calls to have a student leave your class and come to the office. Make up for the time lost and the teaching continuity lost because of the phone call.
32. Maintain your students' concentration despite the loud sounds coming from an adjacent classroom where yet another video is being viewed.
33. Report the very uncomfortable temperature in your classroom to the school administration, but continue teaching despite extreme heat or extreme cold in the classroom.
34. Speak to students as they enter class and when they leave class. Monitor the hallway from your classroom door area during class change times.
35. Deal with students who disobey instructions, who break rules, who disrupt class, who interfere with the work you are doing with your class. Get involvement from a school administrator as needed.
36. Report any extraordinary concern or incident to school authorities when you hear, hear of, or see anything that suggests a student may be experiencing harm, may harm himself or herself, or may harm other people.
37. Enforce the school's dress code. Dress for work as a professional.
38. Notify parents and guardians of great work done by students. Notify parents and guardians of misbehavior by students and of declining grades or failing grades.

39. Keep track of all books distributed to students. Conduct book checks as needed during the school year. Collect all books at the end of the school year. Submit book inventory information as required.
40. Carefully use and manage all equipment in the classroom.
41. Promote and exemplify safe activity in the classroom.
42. Notice and monitor each student throughout each class.
43. _____.

Yes, that list adds up to an abundance of work, of labor, of exertion, of time, and of effort. The highest hopes and the most laudable intentions come face to face with the classroom reality of every skill, task, endeavor, duty, and action that teaching involves.

No classroom can function by automatic pilot, remote control, or momentum from yesterday. Teaching well is physically demanding, mentally draining, emotionally taxing, and just plain difficult. Teaching well is also productive, meaningful, and rewarding.

If the work of teaching appears to be easy and simple, look again and delve into the many specifics that compose the totality of a teacher's duties. It is possible to be an excellent teacher and to cause excellent learning. Diligence is mandatory. Diligent excellence is an earned result and reward.

When a teacher follows and implements the guidance of his or her conscience, diligent excellence is made possible. Idealism does not grade papers. Work grades papers. Be idealistic, but always do the work. Idealism is manifested through diligent work. Such work enables you to obtain diligent excellence.

Chapter Twenty-Eight

Increasing Complexity

People who teach for a career of twenty-five years, thirty years, or longer, may encounter a time when an unexpected reality hits: "This is not the work I signed up for." What happened? What changed? Is something wrong? How did the work a teacher originally signed up to do become such different work that it seems teaching now is an altogether new set of tasks and duties?

Real teaching has not changed. The fundamental characteristics of great teachers one or two generations ago remain as the essential traits of great teachers today. The political system, the bureaucrats, the top-ranking education hierarchy power brokers, and some school administrators increasingly redefine teacher and teaching in ways that are unlike the proven definition, but timeless truths have an inherent, earned authority and value that trendy fads can never attain.

At some unfortunate moment in the past few decades the term *facilitator* began to gain faddish and fashionable momentum as a modern definition of or replacement for the word *teacher*. A conscientious teacher should reject the demotion to facilitator.

To facilitate is to make something easier. A teacher's responsibility is not to make learning easier; rather, a teacher's responsibility is to make learning happen. Learning that has value, worth, substance, and authenticity is not easily obtained. Real learning involves real work.

CASE STUDY 1

"Welcome to everyone. It is wonderful that you can attend our annual education innovation conference. Our theme is Teachers as Facilitators—The Future of the Classroom. Your attendance at this conference confirms your eagerness to make this vital transition from teacher to facilitator. We'll save announcements and other procedures for later. Right now our featured speaker will begin the conference with a magnificent presentation. She prefers to have no introduction, so I'll just say how honored we are to have Samantha Alexandria Hightower with us today."

Guest speaker: Thank you. Thank you for that kind welcome. It is so good to be in your state today. I travel constantly. I'll make this presentation thirty-seven times this summer at conferences such as yours. The ideas you will hear today are the cutting-edge, out-of-the-box ideas that are sweeping across our classrooms throughout the nation. It is time for all of us to join the teacher as facilitator bandwagon.

What is meant by teacher as facilitator? Essentially, teachers will now guide and mentor students instead of directly instruct students. The facilitator model calls for classrooms to become incubators of ideas and for teachers to become advocates for or nurturers of knowledge. The educational facilitator will work with students to share in the creation of activities that stir the imagination of students. The classroom will be a world of guided discovery where students are equal partners and participants.

One example I use is to say that the teacher as facilitator is the director of a theatrical performance. The students are the actors and the actresses. The facilitator guides, coaches, directs, interacts, oversees, and supervises the students. But the students present the performance on the stage, which is the classroom, and the director is not a participant in that performance. Students own their education in this model, and the facilitator helps them shop for it, evaluate options, and then makes the purchase.

Description: The guest speaker's presentation continued for exactly one hour. Samantha Alexandria Hightower had memorized sixty minutes of scripted material. Of course, she included many pictures, key points summarized on a screen, and two short video segments of perfectly behaved students eagerly complying with the perfectly charming direction of a classroom facilitator.

The images shown and the descriptions given made the classroom resemble a child's birthday party where energy and entertainment were in full force but where learning was not a consideration. The facilitators shown in the video segments seemed to be party planners who caused fun instead of teachers who cause learning.

Evaluation: One teacher in the audience texted the following comment to a friend who was also in the audience but sitting on the other side of the 1,500-seat assembly room that was filled beyond capacity, with twenty-four people standing. The text stated, "Why are we here? This is awful. I'm a teacher, not a talent show host. Can you believe people get paid to say this nonsense we're hearing?" The friend replied succinctly: "Makes me sick."

A conscience-driven teacher is not a facilitator. Why? One reason is that students need more than direction, mentoring, and guidance. Students need adults to teach them. As students grow from childhood to adolescence to teenage years they can increasingly accept responsibilities, they can select between a range of options offered by a teacher who is skilled in instructional design, they can contribute to the direction of their education and to the activities of their education, but they need direct instruction from a teacher.

A conscientious teacher knows that even as students mature from elementary school to middle school to high school, the adults are in charge. The adults know the curriculum content that students must master. The vague concept of or nebulous activities of a facilitator do not equal the precise duties of a teacher or the certain activities of teaching.

A temporary trend such as teacher as facilitator may have an idea within it that merits consideration, so some educators may not completely dismiss fads. These optimistic adventurers may think they can distill one good idea out of an overall disastrous concept, and perhaps they can.

The search for good ideas in education is much more productive when the seeker gains wisdom from great teachers whose goals and whose motives are to cause learning. The goals and the motives of people who profit from the latest educational fad or trend may be quite different from causing learning by doing what works best for students.

Trends including the teacher as facilitator can be rejected. Some societal trends cannot be denied, and, therefore, they must be faced realistically. One such societal trend impacting schools is the increased tendency to use schools as the delivery system of solutions to address any problem that impacts the age group in the kindergarten through high school years. Beware.

From childhood nutrition concerns to anger management issues, from dispensing prescription medications to combating drug use, the tasks assigned to schools multiply year after year. The fundamental duty of a school is to cause learning. Letting schools concentrate on academic education while families work with other social structures and organizations to concentrate on other issues can be efficient, orderly, and productive as specific expertise is applied at each service provider.

In the early decades of television, rightful and accurate concerns emerged regarding the number of hours daily that children and teenagers watched the intellectually empty programs on television. In recent years a similar concern has emerged over hours lost by children and teenagers to video games. A more recent problem is the hour after hour spent daily by students with social media, texting, and similar electronic-gadget-led pastimes.

The hours absorbed by television, video games, social media, texting, and cell phone banter can add up to weeks or months not used on more meaningful, beneficial and productive activities. Students who do not turn in homework, students who do not read the assigned reading, students who sleep in class because of late nights texting are students whose teachers still have to educate them.

For this reason and many others, teaching is more complex, more complicated, more challenging, more frustrating, more strenuous, and more problematic than before. Added to the social changes and added to new attention-consuming pastimes of students are the perennial reforms imposed on schools. Teachers can validly wonder if there are ways to successfully counter the antieducation forces that invade schools.

There is no easy answer, but a conscience-driven teacher does have the absolute assurance that her work is important and that his standards are true. Fads fade. Trends do their damage and exit. Education reform continues as one reform fails and another reform is substituted, only to fail also.

In the midst of this apparent abyss the conscience-driven teacher's foundation of character, integrity, honor, virtue, and work ethic combined with a resolve to cause learning will get results. This teacher designs, assembles, provides, and implements an overall classroom experience that gets results for students and with students.

Teaching will continue to be invaded by, raided by, and encroached upon by trends, fads, societal changes, political reforms, and bad decisions by leaders who sometimes mislead or managers who sometimes mismanage. Teaching is complex and demanding today. Teaching will be more complex and more demanding in every following school year.

What is a conscience-driven teacher to do? What does the conscience of a teacher offer to someone who daily faces the challenges within a classroom made more complicated by the turbulent outside forces impacting the classroom?

Be realistic. Know exactly what you are dealing with. Be very aware, and be very well informed.

Do not go it alone. No one person can completely counter the growing intricate and knotty factors impacting education.

Persist. Outlast the fading fads, the temporary trends, the impermanent reforms.

Do what works. Do what has always worked. Do what will always work.

New machines, new technology, new devices will always be introduced to the marketplace. Some of those may be helpful with education. Some of those are a waste of educators' time and money.

Sophisticated, quality, reputable research can offer worthwhile insights and ideas. Filter those insights and ideas through your unique awareness of the classroom conditions where you work.

Following your conscience; honestly evaluating the effectiveness of your instructional methods; trading ideas with colleagues who face a similar classroom reality to the reality you encounter daily; continuing to learn; getting wise advice; taking good care of yourself; knowing your students, their progress, and their academic needs are all within the capability of a conscientious teacher.

You can still shape the destiny of your classroom. You can still be the teacher you intended to be even if schools and society are not what they once were. You, the educator who is led by the conscience of a teacher, are needed more than ever. You also need to be more prepared than ever for harder work and more difficult circumstances than ever.

Chapter Twenty-Nine

Not Alone

"This is worse than last year, and last year was terrible. Why don't students pay attention? Why do they keep trying to sneak out their cell phones during class? They know that is wrong. Why did so many students not turn in the project that was due today? What type of grade do they expect to get? Do they care about their grade? Why do my emails to their parents or guardians get such weak replies or no reply at all? How am I supposed to deal with all of this stuff? It's too much."

A teacher who is expressing those thoughts may think that she is doing something wrong and that other teachers are having much better experiences. The teacher should talk to colleagues and get a gauge on overall conditions in classrooms around the school. The goal is not to complain together; rather, the goal is to express concerns and to learn together. Who is doing what works best in the school? Everyone in the school needs to know what is working well in the most successful classrooms.

A strong conscience does not make a teacher immune to lazy students, irresponsible students, vulgar students, defiant students, disruptive students, incorrigible students, potentially dangerous students, or court-involved students. Dealing with the realities of teaching can break your heart, deplete your energy, lead you to question teaching as a career choice, and fill you with despair. Do not let these toxins fester. Do not go it alone.

When the days of teaching are filled with despair, anxiety, anguish, aggravation, dismay, and letdowns, ask colleagues how they cope with those reactions. What do they do when a day of teaching has more problems than solutions, more failures than successes, more exhaustion than inspiration, more desperation than determination?

Your conscience can remain very healthy as it constantly calls for actions and attitudes based on honor, virtue, good character, ethics, and righteousness. Despite this consistency, clarity, and health of conscience, the mind can become weary, the heart can feel defeated, and the body can be overwhelmed.

A conscientious yet discouraged and exhausted teacher may need to commiserate with colleagues so everyone can acknowledge their pains and tribulations. This is not to form a "woe is me" or "woe are all of us" vortex of victims; rather, this is to express concerns, release anxieties, collectively empathize, and together find solutions.

A struggling teacher may wonder why other people seem so exuberant, so confident, so unbothered in a school that could be described as dysfunctional, chaotic, misled, and mismanaged. Are other people unaware of the unacceptable conditions? Have other people just given up and given in, concluding that nothing can be done? Do other people think the school is doing well when a closer look would reveal serious troubles?

A conscientious teacher is aware, has not given up, will not give in, and evaluates school conditions realistically. The emerging reality can be oppressive or potentially devastating, especially to a lone, solitary crusader. Be not alone in your work as a teacher. Greatness is enhanced through purposeful partnerships. Greatness can be limited by silent suffering in isolation.

"But if I ask for help or support, will I look like a weak teacher?" Only to people whose judgment is flawed. Asking for help or support confirms your eagerness to get results and reveals anew that people multiply their effectiveness when they share ideas, share concerns, work together, and team up.

Is a surgeon weak because he needs a team supporting him in the operating room? Is a chef weak because she needs servers to take the meals to the diners? Is a baseball pitcher weak because he needs a catcher to catch and then return the ball? Is a high school senior weak because she needs help with the process of applying to college?

Each of those questions is answered with *no*. The same reasoning can be applied to a teacher who reaches out for ideas, encouragement, support, or someone to listen. Conscientious teachers give of themselves all day, every day. The reserves of energy, hope, endurance, and resolve can fade or be depleted. Rebuilding those reserves is better done together with other people and is much less likely to occur alone.

Together, not alone, capable, concerned, competent teachers can strengthen each other. What is a struggle for an individual can become a victory for a united group with a shared purpose.

Teaming up with the right people in the right way to achieve the right results is wise. Because much of a teacher's work is done unaided as the only adult in the classroom, other times must be found to interact symbiotically with colleagues. The goal is to cause learning. The goal is not to cause learning as an isolated, independent contractor who insists on doing everything in seclusion.

Together, not alone, is far superior to alone, never together.

Chapter Thirty

Enough?

"There was a time, many years ago, when the dominant thought on my mind was to teach. All my life I wanted to be a teacher. Finally, the day arrived, and there I was in a classroom with my students."

"Before that I worked for a big company. It was just an irresistible opportunity. I had a great employer and endless career possibilities with that company. Teaching could never come close to the income I had. I worked with incredibly talented, smart people. I left all of that to live my dream. I left all of that to grasp the peace that could come from doing what I had always dreamed of doing."

"Now, after decades have passed, I am at a time when the dominant thought on my mind is not to teach. I must end this long, sometimes wonderful, yet increasingly unappealing endeavor. I must admit that it is over. I must leave this behind and move on. Teaching is not what it once was. Did teaching change or did I change or did both change? At this point previous victories cannot be repeated. Maybe that is true with any career in any line of work. Maybe that is just a human cycle. Work changes in good ways and in bad ways, and at some point adaptation is unacceptable and correction is impossible."

"Once it was worth giving up everything to become a teacher. Now, continuing to teach is costing me too much. It has become life threatening. I have no career. The career I chose no longer exists. Maybe my expectations were unrealistic. Maybe teaching needs to change back to what it once was. The career I chose has disappeared. Teaching is no longer teaching. Schools are no longer schools. I cannot fight this battle any longer. Enough of this."

"For those who remain, I applaud you and I caution you. Our working conditions have gone from bad to worse. They could deteriorate from worse to total disaster. If your heart, mind, and soul insist that you teach, then keep teaching. In that case, the classroom is where you belong, it is the only workplace where you belong."

"If your heart, mind, and soul do not unanimously insist that you continue to teach, I advise you to get out. Leave now. Find other employment. You cannot overcome the antieducation forces that are organized against you. It is a lost cause. It will defeat you. It can destroy you. Your survival requires your immediate exit."

"I have seen so many bad decisions made at schools during my career. I have endured the ramifications of bad decisions about education made by principals, school districts, state government, and the national government. Do the people making those decisions ever listen to teachers?"

"I have seen people selected for school administration jobs who had no skills and no abilities. What they did have were friends in the right places. Do those people have no shame? Do they ever realize the damage they cause? How can they have a clear conscience? Why didn't they pick me for one of those positions? I had more skills and experience. I just was never a decision maker's best friend."

"So, I need to go. I have some treasured memories. Hundreds, really thousands of students learned a lot from me. Some other students refused to learn anything. I can honestly say I did my very best. I did everything I could for every student I taught. I'm sixty-one years old. I taught for thirty-two years. Enough."

Cynical? Realistic? Burned out? Frustrated? Declaring victory and moving into a well-deserved retirement? Passing the duty of teaching to the next generation of eager, youthful teachers? A victim of the futility that accompanies career abuse when decision makers repeatedly refused to interview her for school administration work when she was more qualified than the people who were chosen? Weary of working harder and better than other people who were in the principal's inner circle and who got all of the favored treatment?

Be ahead of the enough moment. See it coming. Do not hit the enough moment and have no options. Staying in the classroom as a teacher past the enough moment is harmful. Your conscience will tell you when enough is approaching.

Think hard, deeply, realistically, and with much wise counsel before deciding to earn the credentials to be a teacher. Once you are a teacher, once again think long, hard, deeply, realistically, and with much wise counsel about whether this should be your long-term career.

If you are right for teaching and if teaching is right for you, the career experiences for you and the learning experiences for your students can be monumental, glorious, life touching, and life changing. Listen to your conscience. Honestly evaluate your teaching results and your classroom experiences. Do what is right. Do what you would hope a person who could someday be the teacher of your own children would do.

If you and teaching are not a completely symbiotic match, there will be many regrets. Listen to your conscience. Honestly evaluate your teaching aptitude, results, and your classroom experiences. Do what is right. Do what you would hope a person who could someday teach your own children should do.

Epilogue

Your Conscience Speaks to You

We have known each other for a long time. You sensed my warning during your childhood. I told you to tell your third-grade teacher about the student who you saw steal money from another student. You heard my caution in middle school when your friends spread rumors that almost started a fight, but you told a counselor and the fight was prevented.

In high school you listened to me and you avoided that party following a football game. After the police were called to that party, five people you knew were arrested. You realized that the group having the party should be kept far away from you, and you separated yourself from them forever.

It was not easy, but in your last semester of the five-year college and graduate school program when you were a student teacher, you obeyed my instructions to not attend some late-night campus activities. You knew it was important to be well rested and well prepared for student teaching each morning.

We have worked together for years. I am your conscience, your inner voice of right and wrong. Now that you used my guidance and became a teacher, I can help guide you in your professional work life as I have helped and still will help you in your personal life.

Your parents taught you the big differences between right and wrong. I am their loving voice even though they are miles away.

Your teachers taught you to obey rules and instructions. I am their caring voice although they are years in the past.

Your graduate school class on law and ethics in the teaching profession taught you the legal and ethical standards required of a teacher. I am the content of that class giving you daily reminders.

You and I have a mutual commitment, a permanent bond, an imperative covenant. Yes, we have a contract with each other, but our shared vows transcend the process of fulfilling a contract. We fulfill a glorious, complete devotion to truth itself and to the application of honor.

I am your conscience. I am on your side as I work to keep you on the side of righteousness. I have the highest hopes and the deepest concern for your well-being. I seek to help keep you on the straight and narrow path of honor, of integrity, of virtue, of manners, of ethics, of legality, and of goodness.

You hear me on a morning when teaching in particular or when school in general have made you disgusted, frustrated, and disappointed. My message is not to simplistically think positively; rather, my message is to work purposefully. I am telling you to persist, to go to school today and to do the good work you are fully capable of doing. Do not call in sick when you are not ill. Go in determined and prepared.

I remind you that the student who arrives early to class would appreciate some kind words from you rather than being ignored by one more person.

I urge you to properly oppose bad decisions at school and to present better options in the right way, at the right time on issues you can impact.

You and I are lifetime teammates. My purpose is to prevent problems and to help create meaningful and good achievements. When we work together harmoniously, as we often have, the results are magnificent.

Congratulations on being a teacher. Your students need you. Let's work together more than ever so each day brings more outstanding results. Let's work together so on the most difficult days we remind each other that great results are still possible.

I am your conscience. In some ways I am your forever teacher. That means we are both teachers. There is so much to teach. There is so much to learn. All of that can be done better when we teach together, learn together, work together, and listen closely to each other. Are you listening to me now?

I am your conscience. What am I saying to you right now? What will you do in response to what I am saying?

About the Author

Keen Babbage has thirty-one years of experience as a teacher and administrator in middle school and high school. Also, he has taught in college and in graduate school. He is the author of *911: The School Administrator's Guide to Crisis Management* (1996), *Meetings for School-Based Decision Making* (1997), *High-Impact Teaching: Overcoming Student Apathy* (1998), *Extreme Teaching* (2002, 2014), *Extreme Learning* (2004), *Extreme Students* (2005), *Results-Driven Teaching: Teach So Well That Every Student Learns* (2006), *Extreme Economics* (2007, 2009), *What Only Teachers Know about Education* (2008), *Extreme Writing* (2010), *The Extreme Principle* (2010), *The Dream and Reality of Teaching* (2011), *Reform Doesn't Work* (2012), *The Power of Middle School* (2012), *Teachers Know What Works* (2013), *Life Lessons from Cancer* (2013), *Can Schools Survive* (2014), and *Life Lessons from a Dog Named Rudy* (2014).

www.ingramcontent.com/pod-product-compliance
Lightning Source LLC
Chambersburg PA
CBHW082206230426
43672CB00015B/2917